MW01235909

Practical Steps to the Research Process
for High School

MW01235909

Information Literacy Series

Practical Steps to the Research Process for High School

Deborah B. Stanley

1999
Libraries Unlimited, Inc.
and Its Division
Teacher Ideas Press
Englewood, Colorado

*This research guide is dedicated
to the 1997–1998 teachers of Hoover High School,
Glendale Unified School District,
who willingly collaborated with a newcomer
and to Norma Dick, Barbara Jeffus, and Lindsay Koch
who taught me how to creatively embrace change and manage information.*

Copyright © 1999 Libraries Unlimited, Inc.
All Rights Reserved.
Printed in the United States of America.

No part of this publication may be reproduced, stored in a retrieval
system, or transmitted, in any form or by any means, electronic, me-
chanical, photocopying, recording, or otherwise, without the prior permission of the publisher. An exception is made for individual librarians
and educators, who may make copies of activity sheets for classroom
use in a single school or library. Standard citation information should
appear on each page.

Libraries Unlimited, Inc.
(and Its Division
Teacher Ideas Press)
P.O. Box 6633
Englewood, CO 80155-6633
1-800-237-6124
www.lu.com/tip

Library of Congress Cataloging-in-Publication Data

Stanley, Deborah B.
    Practical steps to the research process for high school / Deborah B. Stanley.
    xvii, 230 p. 22x28 cm. -- (Information literacy series)
    Includes bibliographical references and index.
    ISBN 1-56308-762-6
    I. Library orientation for high school students--United States. I. Title. II. Series.
Z711.2.S72 1999
    027.62'6--dc21   99-050169

Contents

List of Figures

Acknowledgments

A special thanks to my husband for his continued support and encouragement during my long hours of computer work.

Many thanks to Betty Morris who came up unexpectedly and asked, "Have you ever thought of turning this [my California School Library Association presentation] into a book?"

Introduction

A Unique Approach

This guide to the Research Process is a unique four-day diary of scripted research lessons. It is based on a generic concept of research and addresses the ever-increasing need for methods to manage information in a practical way. As a working library media teacher, I have had the opportunity to teach research strategies at all grade levels: elementary school, middle school, and high school. This book is the result of successful adaptations of the Research Process at all three levels, and it presupposes the following:

- Past and present research theories are the "what." This guide is the "how" (*Figure I-1*). It goes beyond explaining *what* research is to *how* to actually teach it. In simple practical ways, this book gives back to library media teachers the concepts of research found in their original training classes.

- The lessons and strategies are all based on authentic teaching experiences. Nothing is hypothetical or simply trial tested; it is the result of ongoing interactions with teachers and students. Therefore, this is a "working" document. I constantly find more interesting or effective ways to present this material and therefore assume the reader will apply these lessons creatively. The purpose is empowerment, not insistence.

- The underlying assumption of all lessons and strategies presented is collaboration. As I often tell my classes when I begin a unit, "I will probably learn as much from you and your teacher as you will learn from these lessons." Because you already own it, you are strongly encouraged to use, adapt, or completely reinvent this material. I do not claim sole ownership of any of these lesson strategies because everything was done in collaboration. We are all here to help each other, with the ultimate goal being student success in managing information and in becoming a productive citizen in the global community. The goal is information literacy!

Literacy

Technology Proficiency

Information Literacy

Content-Area Standard

ELL/Special Modifications

Lifelong Skills

Guide Book Clarification

Content

There are four general sections to this guide book. Only Section II is the actual Research Process.

- Section I: Planning and Preparation
- Section II: The Research Process
- Section III: Application and Accountability
- Section IV: Enrichment and Extension

Section II, Chapters 4 through 9, contains the scripted student lessons adapted to fit into three days of instruction at the high school level. Students begin their own hands-on research on the fourth day—Chapter 10 in Section III—starting with quick directions for efficient access of print and electronic sources and equipment.

Design

Important points, anecdotes, and paraphrased conversations are set off with borders for emphasis.

The sidebar icons represent some of the major trends in educational reform. The point of this book is to demonstrate that the Research Process, when meaningfully integrated into the general school curriculum, can be a "magic bullet" for addressing and applying these educational trends. The icons appear throughout the book to support and demonstrate this powerful claim.

Education can greatly benefit from instruction in the Research Process. Therefore, schools need library media teachers at all levels who function as both instructional partners (peers) and educational innovators (leaders) in the push toward information literacy. Whether you agree with this diary of strategies or not, try it, adapt it, and at least come away saying, "I know a much better way to do this." Then do it!

Problem Solving

Fig. I-1. Managing a World of Information

What General Research Is	How the Research Process Works
Teacher Assignment	
Topic Selection (Thesis Statement)	How do I choose a topic? How do I focus my topic?
Select/Evaluate Sources (Primary vs. Secondary Print and Nonprint)	How do I manage so many kinds of sources?
Notetaking Instruction	How do I take notes?
Library Research	How can I read for comprehension?
Outline Information	How do I organize my notes to write?
Rough Draft	
Cite Sources	How do I understand MLA?
Final Draft	How do I write a final bibliography?
Final Bibliography	
Enrichment/Presentation	How do I enrich my project with technology, art, etc.?
Points/Grade Rubric/Authentic Assessment	How can research be tracked and evaluated effectively?

From *Practical Steps to the Research Process for High School* © 1999 Libraries Unlimited. 800-237-6124.

Section 1

Planning and Preparation

 ## Chapter 1
What Is the Research Process?

 ## Chapter 2
Collaborative Planning

 ## Chapter 3
Teaching Preparations

Chapter 1

What Is the Research Process?

"Do all of the students get these lessons? I wish I'd known this when I was in high school."
—Substitute teacher

Fig. 1-1. Research Process

Topic
A. Locate topic ideas in grade-level texts, unit concepts, current literature studies.
B. Check in the library media center for sources to determine supporting information.
C. Cross-check in an encyclopedia to narrow or broaden a topic.
D. Create a thesis statement to investigate the topic.

Subtopics
A. Ask yourself: What do I want to know about my topic?
B. Specific: Pre-search encyclopedia or nonfiction book's table of contents for ideas.
C. General:
    Thing: who, what, when, where, why/how.
    Person: early life, education, accomplishments, later life.
D. Minimum of three subtopics; maximum is determined by time and information.
E. List subtopics in outline form by Roman numeral. Construct outline guide.

Sources
A. Source: Anything used for information.
    Format of sources:
        Print: books, references, magazines, newspapers, maps, charts, etc.
        Nonprint: videos, software, CD-ROMs, Internet.
B. Number of formats (minimum of three). Number of sources.
C. Credit sources using an official guide such as the MLA Bibliography sheet.
D. Know the difference:
    Primary vs. secondary sources.
    Regular vs. annotated bibliography.

Read/Think/Select
A. Read an entire "chunk" *before* selecting facts. Put your pencil down!
B. Think about what was read. What was important?
C. Select appropriate information from each "chunk."

Notetake
A. Note cards: One note per card! Title cards with subtopics.
B. Notebook Paper: Bullet or mark each note. Do not number notes at this time.
C. Record only important facts or keywords.
D. Discard small words like *a*, *an*, and *the*. Use commas and dashes instead.
E. No sentences!
F. Use quotation marks when copying. Give credit with source and page number.
G. Alternative information gathering includes paraphrasing or summarizing.

Sort and Number Notes
A. Sort notes by subtopic, by paragraph ideas, and then by supporting details (outline).
B. Read all your notes. Select good notes; discard irrelevant notes.
C. Sequence notes for fluent writing.
D. Number all notes consecutively from section to section.

Extension
    Write/Publish/Present
    Final bibliography
    Technology integration

Evaluation

The Research Process

Another Theory?

There are many popular theories and methods of information management. It is important that the Research Process (*Figure 1-1*) is not offered as a broad generalization but is a specific process which embodies practical steps exclusively for student research by identifying strategies taught at each step. The purpose of the Research Process is:

- **to reflect** generic concepts of information management intuitively understood by teachers and students and interpret them into easily understandable, specific strategies.

- **to endorse** current popular theories of research because they too are based on generic concepts of accessing, evaluating, and using information, known as information management.

- **to empower** teachers and library media teachers with something they already know but perhaps have been hard pressed to apply for lack of simple, effective strategies.

- **to distill** the complex into something simple: Namely, to contextualize strategies for literacy (*Figure 1-2*) and technology (*Figure 1-3*) into content-area, standards-based, units of study through collaborative lessons. These strategies for student-centered, inquiry-structured research are presented to students at simple and appropriate learning levels engaging them in meaningful and challenging information management experiences. Less is more!

- **to teach** students to think! Each step of the Research Process involves specific strategies to manage information. Learning to navigate the ocean of information is information literacy. The more students perform the strategies, the more adept they become at logical thinking patterns which can be applied in later situations. This is lifelong learning.

Managing information is more than hardware or software instructions. It's like hitting a home run. It requires the learning and practicing of logical strategies to make something easy to do.

Information Literacy

Content-Area Standard

Lifelong Skills

Fig. 1-2. Integrating Literacy

LMT/Teacher	Student
Collaborative planning successfully incorporates all aspects of literacy into units of study. • Reading • Writing • Listening • Speaking	Readability of sources of information is essential so "basic concepts" are accessible for learning to take place. Levels to consider: • Primary language • Grade • Age • Interest • Special needs and/or abilities
Day 1 Lesson • Topic • Subtopics	Reads to determine if there is enough accessible, available information to select and support topic and subtopics.
Day 2 Lesson • Sources	Reads in a variety of print and nonprint formats including: • Books • Internet • References • Internet-based • Magazines search tools • Newspapers • CD-ROMs • Pamphlets • Videos • Maps, charts, graphs • Computer software
Day 3 Lesson • Read/Think/Select	Reads from the sources to access information. (Validates reading and/or listening skills.) Reads for comprehension using special reading-for-research strategies. Reads to evaluate and relate information to topic and subtopics.
• Notetake	Reads to select and record notes: keywords, quotations, paraphrase, summarize.
• Sort/Number Notes	Reads notes to sort, sequence, and number them.
Extension Activities: • Write/Publish/Present • Final bibliography • Technology enrichment	Reads sequenced notes to write a rough draft. (Validates writing skills.) Reads the rough draft to revise, edit, and write a final draft.
Evaluation	Reads the final draft for oral presentation. (Validates speaking skills.) Reads entries to write final bibliography.

From *Practical Steps to the Research Process for High School* © 1999 Libraries Unlimited. 800-237-6124.

Fig. 1-3. Integrating Technology

Research Process Lessons	LMT/Teacher	Student
	Instructional/Mentor Level: • Technology proficiency	Personal Level: • Technology proficiency
Day 1 Lesson • Topic • Subtopics	Creates interesting student handouts using: • Word processing • Desktop publishing • Graphics/Charts	Pre-searches topic/ subtopics using: • Internet • CD-ROMs • Computer software

Day 2 Lesson
• Sources
	• Creates hardware and software pathfinders.
	• Creates signage.
	• Orientations for:
	    Internet
	    CD-ROMs
	    Computer software
		Accesses/locates info. using:
		• Internet
		• Internet-based search tools
		• CD-ROMs
		• Computer software

Day 3 Lesson • Read/Think/Select		• Evaluates printouts from any of the above to process info.: read, comprehend, evaluate, select.
• Notetake		• Records keywords, facts, quotes.
• Sequence Notes		• Uses notepad function of electronic encyclopedias.
Extension Activities: • Write/Publish/Present • Final bibliography • Technology enrichment **Evaluation**	• Tracking sheets • Evaluation reports • Lesson database • Project samples • Technology fair • Electronic inventory • LMC web site	• Word processing • Desktop publishing • Multimedia presentations • Color scanner • Digital camera • Video camera

From *Practical Steps to the Research Process for High School* © 1999 Libraries Unlimited. 800-237-6124.

Fig. 1-4. Approaches to Information Management

Bloom's Taxonomy	BIG 6™ Eisenberg/Berkowitz	5 A's © Ian Jukes	Research Process
Knowledge ↓	Task Definition ↓	Asking ↓	Topic
			Subtopics
	Information Seeking Strategies	Accessing ↓	Sources ↓
	Location & Access		
Comprehension	Use of Information ↓	Analyzing ↓	Read, Think, Select
Application		Applying ↓	Notetake
Analysis			Sort & Number Notes
Synthesis	Synthesize		
Evaluation	Evaluate	Assessing	

The BIG 6™, 1987 copyright of Michael Eisenberg and Bob Berkowitz. Reprinted by permission.
"5 A's," from *NetSavvy II* is used by permission of Ian Jukes, Anita Dosaj, and Bruce Macdonald. Corwin Press, 1999.

From *Practical Steps to the Research Process for High School* © 1999 Libraries Unlimited. 800-237-6124.

Do You See the Connections?

Were you lucky enough to have had a teacher in elementary or middle school who actually taught students that research had steps? Did they understand research enough themselves to explain how to locate information in a source, how to record facts on a million little note cards, and how to write a real bibliography? Even more important, did they not only teach those steps but also allow instructional time for students to perform them? Even if you didn't have a person like this in your past, you can still *become* that person.

Important Idea

Thank you, Mrs. Thornton, my sixth grade social studies teacher. From middle school to high school, from college to grad. school, no one else ever actually taught me research! I could not have been the student I was then, or the teacher I am now, without you!

When you went through the classes for certification for library media teacher, did an instructor have you develop a collaborative unit? In that unit, were you required to develop research strategies (information literacy) integrated into a content area, resulting in a meaningful student product that included technology integration? If so, you must have devised your own version of what you see in this book.

My training began at a time when current theories reflected in *Figure 1-4* were not yet well known. We wrote our first practice units using intuitive concepts of research. In other words, we figured it out! Bloom's Taxonomy enjoyed great popularity in the 1980s as a wave of critical thinking instruction swept our educational environment. It figured strongly into the classroom teaching at that time but was not directly tied into research training. It took Eisenberg and Berkowitz to fully utilize Bloom's work in their "BIG 6" approach to information management, and it was later reintroduced by Ian Jukes in the mid-1990s in his "5 A's" guide to research.

With certificate in hand, when confronted with the reality of managing a school's busy library media center, did the demands of the job overshadow the inclination for you to apply research theories? Now, the power of information literacy puts us all back in the hot seat to revive those graduate school research unit strategies and use them, perhaps in new and different ways.

Perhaps that is why conferences are filled with library media teachers who know all the theories but are asking, "What am I supposed to *do*?" Of course, the answer is: Teach the Research Process!

How Do You Eat an Elephant?

This is the bottom line: If you're a library media teacher, do you teach? If not, what are the overwhelming issues (the "elephants") that are preventing collaborative planning and teaching from occurring?

Time

Juggling our many jobs is the daily plight of the library media teacher. We are pulled in so many different directions. For those of you who are alone in the library media center, without the support services of a clerk or technician, booking most of the periods of your day for direct instruction is out of the question. There is simply no way you can schedule collaborative planning and teaching time and still perform all the other routine management activities of a busy facility. **Time** is your overwhelming "elephant," and there's nothing that will give you more hours in your day. Teaching the Research Process to students will remain on your "Get Real" list until funding, or people, support you. Or, just maybe, there is something else that might assist you: a method.

Money

Many library media teachers are running a facility that has not yet been automated for circulation, much less wired for Internet or CD-ROM tower networking. For many others who have small budgets but large numbers of students who are "literacy challenged," updating your collection to meet curriculum standards precludes the purchase of expensive electronic sources. For you, the variety of information formats in the "Sources" step of the Research Process will remain on your wish list. **Money** for current resources, either print or electronic, is your "elephant." You may be trapped into time-consuming fund raising through grant writing, pleading for digital high school funds, appealing to parent clubs, organizing library activities, etc. Who has time to teach?

Training

Library media teachers just entering the field, and even those who have been around for a while, find they are expected to be media experts. It takes years to learn the many hardware and software technologies, much less the Internet, which we must pull together to model for our colleagues. For many LMTs, technology **training** is the "elephant."

LMTs are expected to be Jacks-of-all-trades, but often we are the masters of none. The reality—the good news—is that we don't have to master everything. We just need to have a wide variety of basic, transferable technology skills, as we saw in *Figure 1-3.*

> *"I'm going to get you started on this program (or piece of equipment), and then I want to see how quickly you can begin to teach me things about it."*
>
> —*LMT to Students*

You

There are many LMTs who seem to have it all: full-time paid support personnel, a budget for books, funds for technology hardware and software, technology prowess that even has them designing web sites, a supportive administrator, great rapport with fellow faculty members, and enthusiasm for the job, yet collaborative teaching just isn't happening. Maybe the science teacher says, "I just need two days in the library media center for my classes to find resources for our project on classification systems," or the English teacher asks, "My students know what they need, can we come for a few days to locate some sources of literary criticism?" And you're so busy juggling other tasks that collaborative teaching has to wait until "next time."

For you, the "elephant" is... **you**. The school thinks you're wonderful, and you are! But the puzzle pieces are still floating in the air. You haven't found that simple system that lets the pieces fall, magically assembled, onto the board. The purpose of this book is to offer the idea that, with your own "spin," the Research Process presented here is the library media teacher's solution to information management: breaking research down into digestible, do-able, bites.

How do you eat an elephant? One bite at a time.

The Missing Link

But what about the students? What does the Research Process mean for them? How many times have you heard a classroom teacher say,

"Our big project of the semester is a research report and presentation on the Vietnam War. Here is a detailed project guide. Notice the list of topic ideas to help you get started. Pay attention to the amount of points possible for each section. Are there any questions? This should be pretty clear. We have a few days of library time scheduled. I'm here to help, but everything is due in two weeks."

Quite unintentionally, and because they're not trained as library media teachers, teachers often confuse the *parts* of a research paper or project for the *strategies* needed to accomplish those parts (*Figure 1-5*). They carefully explain to students what is expected for the title page, the body of the report, the bibliography, the illustrations and footnotes but do not give instructions for choosing an appropriate topic, locating appropriate sources, reading the sources strategically, selecting and recording genuine notes, and writing a report or creating a presentation from those notes. Do we really wonder why kids copy?

Fig. 1-5. Process vs. Project

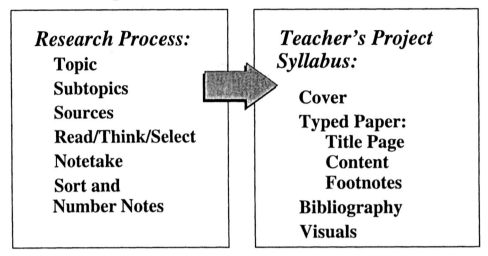

Research Process:	Teacher's Project Syllabus:
Topic	
Subtopics	Cover
Sources	Typed Paper:
Read/Think/Select	Title Page
Notetake	Content
Sort and	Footnotes
Number Notes	Bibliography
	Visuals

From *Practical Steps to the Research Process for High School* © 1999 Libraries Unlimited. 800-237-6124.

I believe the same "missing link" exists for students as it does for instructors. Without instruction, students cannot magically perform genuine research on their own. This brings us back to the question: What is research for students?

What It Is

The Research Process is a series of logical strategies to manage information: accessing, evaluating, and using.

What It Is Not

Logical does not mean self-taught. Each step of the Research Process makes perfect sense, once someone is *shown* how to do it!

As a high school student packed his backpack after a research lesson one day, he said to me, "I'm glad you came to our school. You're really teaching us something." My heart skipped a beat. I knew the research lessons were working!

The Total Package

From the standpoint of the classroom teacher, the library media teacher, and the student, the Research Process is presented here as a package (*Figure 1-6*) that brings together the enormous mandates that true educational reform demands of everyone: the call for literacy, the need for technology integration, accountability for the teaching and learning of content-area standards, and the teaching of information literacy as lifelong skills. These floating puzzle pieces fall, harmoniously assembled, onto the board through the collaboration between the classroom teacher and the library media teacher to teach the Research Process. It exemplifies the "Powerful Teaching and Learning" which educators are called upon to model: hands-on, student-centered, discovery-based, and meaningful.

Fig. 1-6. Powerful Teaching and Learning

Content-Area Standard
 	
ELL/Special Modifications
	Day 1 Lesson
	    Topics
	
	      Subtopics
		The source of appropriate topics is content-area standard units of study.
		
		Choice of topic and numbers of subtopics are modifications for ELL and special students.

Information Literacy **Technology Proficiency**	**Day 2 Lesson** **Sources**	Accessing, evaluating, and crediting a variety of print and electronic sources is a key element of information literacy and reinforces student technology proficiencies. Number, difficulty, and primary language sources are ELL and special student modifications.

Literacy
 	
Problem Solving
	Day 3 Lesson
	    Read/Think/Select
	
	    Notetake
	
	    Sort/Number Notes
		Reading for comprehension is literacy.
		
		Thinking about facts for notetaking by evaluating information is problem solving.
		
		Sorting good from bad notes, then prioritizing and numbering notes for writing is problem solving.

Lifelong Skill	**Extension Activities**
	    Write/Publish/Present
	    Final Bibliography
	    Technology Integration
		Any time a student learns any of the Research Process techniques to gather, organize, and present information, they are learning lifelong skills for information management.

	Evaluation	

From *Practical Steps to the Research Process for High School* © 1999 Libraries Unlimited. 800-237-6124.

Chapter 2

Collaborative Planning

"I don't have a lot of time to plan."
—Classroom teacher

"That's okay. I'll catch you at lunch."
—LMT

Making Time for Collaborative Planning

Undoubtedly, the first step in the Research Process is planning, but how many of you have found that this first hurdle is indeed a high one? Have you heard colleagues say any of the following?

> *"I don't have time to cover my own curriculum. Planning a unit with the library media teacher is one more layer I can't fit in."*
>
> *"Can't I use the library the way I would like? Why do I have to plan with the library media teacher?"*
>
> *"I'm just not the planning kind of person. I need spontaneity!"*
>
> *"I just need library time. My students already know what they need to look for."*

Sound familiar? You are not alone. For the LMT, an important first step toward initiating meaningful planning with teacher colleagues is to become accessible, while eliminating barriers. How do you present yourself and your desire to teach information literacy lessons to teachers who may be resistant to change, or who simply say, "I don't have time"?

The Microwave Oven Syndrome

Important Idea

Offer teachers something they don't know they can't live without!

- Call yourself a *library media teacher* instead of a librarian, so fellow teachers get the clear message you are a certified faculty member. Call the library media center your "classroom!"

- Create a handout of information literacy standards (*Figure 15-1*, p. 216), so fellow teachers understand that while you have your own curriculum, it is never taught in isolation. In fact, it will enhance their program through meaningful integration into content-area units of study.

- Get to work on genuine lesson plans, not just instruction sheets to operate hardware and software. Create research forms on your computer, or adapt them from this guide book, so you can digitally tweak lessons to meet each teacher's needs.

Billboard Yourself

Important Idea

Do your fellow teachers even know the library media program has its own standards and curriculum, called information literacy? You are your own best advertisement. Literally billboard yourself and the information management strategies you are preparing to teach. Choose one good colleague with whom to plan and teach that first set of lessons. Create a wall-size mural documenting the sequence of lessons and activities. To do that, choose a color scheme and attractively matte and paste, in sequential order, each day's research or activity forms, supported by actual student work. Enliven it with snapshots of students pre-searching for topic and subtopic ideas, locating and accessing a variety of sources, reading for comprehension, taking notes, writing a rough draft, and adding technology enhancements to their finished product.

Sell Yourself

Whenever a teacher comes to schedule library time, take them to the mural and walk them through each step of the Research Process. They will quickly realize this is something they haven't been covering with their students. "You do this?" they'll ask. Not only this, you'll explain how you adapt each step of the Research Process to exactly fit their content-area requirements, time constraints, or special needs students.

Support Teaching Styles

Just as a doctor needs a great bedside manner to be really effective, the library media teacher needs to "read" each teacher's personality and instructional style and adapt or offer services accordingly. Learn teachers' differences, then match the time and complexity of planning accordingly. The popular theme "Unity Through Diversity" may be the most positive approach to the unique role of the library media teacher in dealing with every teacher on a campus. In other words, channel their differences in teaching styles, and their willingness to collaborate, into creative and positive experiences for you both.

Adjust

Hitting everyone with the entire Research Process isn't always appropriate. The Spanish teacher may find that his first experience with you in the fall doesn't have to be a fully planned lesson at all, but just a quick, "Hey, I found a great new web site for cultural awareness that your class might enjoy letting me demonstrate." Making yourself accessible in order to initiate planning with staff members is a simple way to get started. I guarantee better things will follow! The following sections offer other techniques to encourage LMT accessibility yet balance the demands on your time with the needs of your diverse clientele.

The Role of the LMC Master Calendar

Toss out the planning book! The key word here is "book." A book is a barrier. Would you go into another teacher's classroom and write something in *their* planning book? Do you go into your spouse's wallet or purse? There are some assumed boundaries we're all hesitant to cross. Instead, grab that desk mat calendar. You know, the one they handed out free at the beginning of the year. Stick a couple of tacks into the most accessible bulletin board or wall space in the library media center. Find the spot that everyone must pass on their way to the faculty meeting. Presto! The next thing you'll hear is,

"Hey, can I just sign myself up, so my classes can get on the computers?" asks the history teacher.

"Sure," you reply "Just use a pencil, in case your plans change later."

Important Idea

A wall calendar is a very friendly, inviting, and open means of scheduling. The buy-in is instant and tremendous because teachers feel they are scheduling for what's already theirs—the library. I found this simple device quite by accident, a few years ago. I knew that, due to new job opportunities for my family, I would be resigning at the end of the school year. I also knew that the LMT position would not necessarily be funded the following year. Although I initiated a variety of strategies to enable a smooth transition to a teacher-run facility, the wall chart for self-scheduling became the overwhelming favorite. Suddenly I had solved all those scheduling problems had plagued me for years. The teachers took to it instantly, and I've used it every year since! Here are some simple calendar guidelines which are born of experience and tested by time:

Color Coding

Red: Unchangeable district data such as school holidays.

Blue: Unchangeable school site data such as staff development days and situations where the school site books the library media center for meetings or events.

Green: Unchangeable LMT obligations such as on- or off-site meetings and conferences.

Pencil: All teacher sign-ups. The ability to erase is essential!

Aligning the Calendars

Using all other official calendars, the library media teacher fills in the red, blue, and green sections. Be sure to sufficiently block out the calendar days for district and site schedule interruptions so that teachers do not mistakenly schedule over them. However, the LMT's personal commitments may not interfere with some LMC activities. Therefore, I draw a green box around my meeting times, leaving the interior of the box available for teacher sign-ups. Once I began this system, I quite literally never had another scheduling foul-up, except when I overcommitted myself!

Signing Up

Buy-in to the library media program will be a bountiful harvest resulting from sowing the seeds of ownership. Teacher self-sign-ups convey to your colleagues that it is truly everyone's library media center providing a variety of services including those of a library media teacher. Using an LMT is a choice, not an obligation. It is remarkable how much they will begin to seek you out when they see the wonderful things you did with another class. "I want to do that too!" is a sign of successful empowerment.

Although teachers sign up freely, I indeed try to catch everyone. Face-to-face dialog is an outreach opportunity I obsessively snag. While a teacher is signing up on the calendar and asking me about the coding directions, I may slip in, "By the way, let me know if I can assist you with anything when you bring your class in. Has your class had an Internet orientation yet?"
The teacher's subject area determines whether I offer research lessons. In high school, sticking to science and/or history classes helps prevent student research lesson duplication.

Fig. 2-1. Calendar Directions

Calendar

Record in pencil this information:

Name   Grade   *Code   Unit topic

*Codes

- (B) Book checkout
- (R) Research time with LMT
- (I) Internet
- (SM) Self-monitored group

From *Practical Steps to the Research Process for High School* © 1999 Libraries Unlimited. 800-237-6124.

Post the Directions

In high school, this calendar may actually become your lesson plans! Therefore, as you can see in *Figure 2-1*, coming up with simple ways to convey complex information is essential. When you also remember the ultimate goal is to remove barriers for teachers, then the quick codes you see on a busy day (*Figure 2-2*) become even more important.

Fig. 2-2. Busy Calendar Day

Periods			Date
0 Jenkins Ⓑ ESL		**2**	
1 Flanery (R-SM)	Mrs. Smith I Bio		
2 Jenkins Ⓑ ESL	Jimenez 9 Ⓡ Day 1 WWII		
3 Flanery (R-SM)	Jimenez 9 Ⓡ Day 1 WWII		
4			
5 Flanery (R-SM)	Jimenez 9 Ⓡ Day 1 WWII		
6 Flanery (R-SM)	Jimenez 9 Ⓡ Day 1 WWII		

Pencils Only

"And no erasing of anyone's name but your own!" you remind teachers with a wink. If your LMC calendar often seems like Grand Central Station, pencil is the surest way to keep the trains from colliding. Does this next situation sound familiar?

On Friday, Mrs. X signs up her five classes for two full days of Internet research. She stops back in on Monday, all in a flurry, and wants to change to next week because the chemistry experiments haven't been completed yet. "Just erase," I say. "Mr. Z came in a moment ago and will be glad to take your place." Isn't a happy staff wonderful?! You may not be able to meet everyone's needs all the time, but with a pencil and an eraser, you can come pretty close.

Fig. 2-3. Lesson Plan Template

UNIT/LESSON TOPIC: _____

Teacher: _____

Project: _____

Grade: _____ #Students: _____ Periods: _____ #Days: _____

LMT's Information Skills	Teacher's Content Skills/Goals
1. Topic: 2. Subtopics: 3. Number/Kinds of sources: 4. Number of notes: 5. Note modification: 6. Sort and number notes: 7. Technology:	1. 2. 3. 4. 5. 6. 7. 8.
LMT Preparation	**Teacher Preparation**
_____ Collaboratively plans unit/lesson with teacher. _____ Provides Lesson Plan Template. _____ Prepares student packet. _____ Previews/locates resources. _____ Collaboratively guides students through Research Process, teaching lessons with information literacy. _____ Provides as-needed technology instruction and assistance. _____ Other:	_____ Meets with LMT to plan unit. _____ Prepares unit syllabus. _____ Assists with suggesting or locating resources. _____ Pre-teaches unit concepts. _____ Tracks students progress through Research Process. _____ Monitors on-task behavior and student discipline. _____ Other:

From *Practical Steps to the Research Process for High School* © 1999 Libraries Unlimited. 800-237-6124.

Let's Do Lunch

Creating accessible planning time between classroom teachers and the library media teacher can often make or break a program, yet optimal planning time with teachers rarely seems to exist. Solution: Let them pick the time and the place. If that falls short, simply catch them at lunch! Rather than feeling interrupted, teachers are usually just as glad not to have to make another meeting time.

The trick is speed and simplicity. Model efficient planning, and teachers will come back again and again. This is accomplished by devising a simple template, such as *Figure 2-3*, in your computer but never ask a teacher to fill it in! Remember those barriers we're trying to eliminate? You don't even need to carry it with you when you finally catch that elusive teacher. You already know what to ask because remembering what's on the template equips you with the basic questions.

While sitting at lunch, reach into the middle of the table, grab a napkin, and jot down the lesson information from your conversation. Type it into the computer yourself when you get back to your desk (see *Figure 2-4*). This is not more work for you when you weigh this small effort against the template's big advantages. The template:

- *provides "at a glance" basic lesson or unit information.*

- *clearly defines separate roles and responsibilities for both the teacher and the LMT, to ensure true collaboration.*

- *provides a generic database adaptable to every teacher's needs.*

- *allows the LMT quick turn-around time from inputting data to giving back to the teacher a "working" lesson plan.*

- *provides a quick way to alter and improve lessons following a final debriefing at the conclusion of the project.*

- *provides a repository of polished lessons for site review or accreditation, grant writing, and networking with other library media teachers.*

Fig. 2-4. Sample Completed Lesson Plan

UNIT/LESSON TOPIC: <u>World War II</u>

Teacher: <u>John Doe</u>

Project: Report of information with oral presentation

Grade: <u>10th</u> **#Students:** <u>32-36 per class</u> **Periods:** <u>1, 3, 4, 5, 6</u> **#Days:** <u>5 or more</u>

LMT's Information Skills	Teacher's Content Skills/Goals

1. **Topic:** person, battle, choices
2. **Subtopics:** Minimum 3
   General: see guide sheet
   Specific: pre-search in sources
3. **Number/Kinds of sources:** 3 formats, 5 sources Primary and/or secondary:
   • Books   • References
   • CD-ROM   • Internet
4. **Number of notes:**
   10 per day, 50 total
5. **Note modification:** ELL as needed
6. **Sort and number notes:** in class
7. **Technology:**
   • Electronic card catalog
   • CD-ROM/Internet
   • Word processing
	1. **Literacy:** Students read from variety of formats of information.
	2. **Standards:**
	   • Social science: World War II
	   • Technology proficiencies
	   • Communication
	   • Information literacy
	3. **Writing:** report of information
	4. **Geography:** World War II locations
	5. **Final report requirements:**
	   • Typed
	   • Attractive cover
	   • Title page
	   • 5 pages content, minimum
	   • Final annotated bibliography
	   • Visual images: picture, map, etc.

LMT Preparation	**Teacher Preparation**
_____ Collaboratively plans unit/lesson with teacher _____ Provides Lesson Plan Template. _____ Prepares student packet. _____ Previews/locates resources. _____ Collaboratively guides students through Research Process, teaching lessons with information literacy. _____ Provides as-needed technology instruction and assistance. _____ Tracking: Assists teacher with daily student accountability.	_____ Meets with LMT to plan unit. _____ Prepares unit syllabus. _____ Assists with sugesting or locating resources. _____ Pre-teaches unit concepts. _____ Tracks students' progress through Research Process. _____ Monitors on-task behavior and student discipline. _____ Tracking: Daily student accountablity for sources and notes.

From *Practical Steps to the Research Process for High School* © 1999 Libraries Unlimited. 800-237-6124.

Purposeful Planning

Content-Area Standard

It is during the planning stage for Research Process instruction that the library media teacher has perhaps the greatest chance to impact the school's instructional program.

- Push toward educational reform by modeling collaboration.

- Teach information literacy through sequential strategies.

- Align print and electronic resources with curriculum standards.

- Promote literacy for purpose and for pleasure.

- Support staff and student technology proficiencies through technology integration into research lessons.

All other areas of the curriculum have their own standards, but information literacy standards are only meaningfully taught through the content of the other subject areas. What drives what? Do the information literacy standards drive the need for literacy and technology integration, or does the mandate for schools to teach literacy and technology drive the need for a library media teacher who can effectively spearhead information literacy instruction? If the answer is "Yes" to one or the other, or both, the underlying mandate is for the LMT to be an active teaching partner. Therefore, the library media teacher assumes the vital role of "change agent" and should, at the very minimum, strive to fulfill the three parts of the title:

Literacy

Library: Plan to meaningfully integrate print resources into units of study. All students should have access to reading materials that are age, grade, subject, language, and interest appropriate.

Technology Proficiency

Media: Plan to meaningfully integrate technology into units of study. A wide variety of technology hardware, software, and networking services are never taught in isolation, as in the old days of "library skills," but are embedded in teachers' units of study through all steps of the Research Process. Be innovative as well as resourceful.

Information Literacy

Teacher: Collaboratively plan to teach information literacy through the Research Process. The LMT does more than point to the location of information and give instructions on the operation of hardware and information software. Be a teacher as well as a facilitator.

Fig. 2-5. LMT: Change Agent for the 21st Century

Library

- Literature promotion.
- Facility management.
- Equitable access to a variety of sources.
- Selection, weeding of the collection.
- Cataloging, processing decisions.
- Daily circulation overview.

Media

- Hardware: computers, scanner, digital camera, laser disk player, modem, AV equipment.
- Software: word processing, desktop publishing, CD-ROMs.
- Networking: Internet, e-mail.

Teacher

- Collaboration in lesson design and instruction of the Research Process.
- Integration of technology into content-area units of study.
- Instructional partner to achieve standards-based site achievement goals.
- Empowering agent for literacy and information literacy.

From *Practical Steps to the Research Process for High School* © 1999 Libraries Unlimited. 800-237-6124.

Chapter 3

Teaching Preparations

"Thanks for the packet of research forms. I can teach most of this myself when the library is booked."

—Collaborating teacher

Fig. 3-1. Research Process: Three Lessons

Day 1 Lesson **Part 1: Topic**	**Lesson 1 objectives** • Where do topics come from? • What makes a topic good? • Matching the topic to the student. • Resources to help identify topics.
Part 2: Subtopics	• Why this is the most important part of the Research Process. • Ask: "What do you want to know about your topic?" • Factors that determine the number of subtopics, and why this is important. • How to use subtopics to modify for special students.
Day 2 Lesson **Sources**	**Lesson 2 objectives** • The difference between sources and formats. • Factors that determine the number of sources and the number of formats. • Why research can never be based on only one source. • What is copyright? • What is a bibliography, and where do they come from? • Hands-on activity to create MLA bibliography entries for three formats.
Day 3 Lesson **Part 1: Read/Think/Select**	**Lesson 3 objectives** • Read for comprehension. • Think about what's important. • Select information to support topic and match subtopics.
Part 2: Notetake	• What are notes? • What makes a note good or bad. • Other forms of information gathering.
Part 3: Sort and Number Notes	• Three steps for prioritizing notes: reading, evaluating (selecting/sequencing), numbering.

From *Practical Steps to the Research Process for High School* © 1999 Libraries Unlimited. 800-237-6124.

Research Instruction

How Many Lessons?

During the planning meeting, the library media teacher and the classroom teacher divided responsibilities and understood what each would do to begin preparation for the upcoming research unit. The library media teacher will prepare information literacy lesson and activity forms, namely templates in this guide book. The amount of materials is based on the number of lessons multiplied by the number of students.

If there are six steps in the Research Process, are there six lessons? Wouldn't it be nice at the high school level if time permitted the luxury of covering the material that thoroughly? But we all know that if you asked even your best friend to team up with you for six lessons, and that didn't include hands-on research time, collaborative teaching would die at conception. In high school I learned that if time is the mother of effective strategies, then maximum efficiency is the father of the research which is actually accomplished. The two can be easily blended into the teaching of effective research strategies in just three lessons (*Figure 3-1*). Each of the goals and objectives for the three lessons will be fully explained in following chapters. Meanwhile, the student handouts for these three lessons, assembled as a packet at the end of this chapter, are only a part of the library media teacher's preparations.

Preparing the Setting

Facility

Since the first three days of research instruction fall primarily on the shoulders of the library media teacher, the logical setting for instruction is the library media center. It is important to set a tone for students that this facility is a purposeful "hub of information," as well as a source of literature for pleasure reading. Ideally, schools that have newer or remodeled library facilities have a classroom immediately adjacent to the LMC solely for instructional purposes.

Signage

Lacking an adjacent classroom, signage can be used effectively to simply block off an instructional section of the main room. That way, other classes and students can freely come and go in other areas. The obvious drawback is distraction and noise. This can be particularly troublesome for research classes with less mature students who are easily distracted under the best of circumstances. The solution lies in good collaborative planning. First, any teacher sharing the LMC has signed up on the calendar, so there are no surprises. Second, arrange for good crowd control with both the collaborating and the independent teachers. Strict behavior rules are in effect as in any classroom.

Information Literacy

Information Literacy

Literacy

Fig. 3-2. Sample LMC Table Sign

From *Practical Steps to the Research Process for High School* © 1999 Libraries Unlimited. 800-237-6124.

Pre-teaching preparations include creating table signs which say, "RESERVED" *(Figure 3-2)*. Quick and easy: print them out from the computer on bright neon paper, laminate two signs back to back, and slip them over a bookend placed in the middle of each table. That way it's easy to say to the incoming class, "Please take a seat at the tables reserved for you." The signs can be quickly removed if the next period is not being used for instruction.

Classroom Alternatives

There are times when the library media center may be better utilized by classes or groups of students working independently, particularly if technology stations are in demand. Therefore, in some cases it may be just as effective for the library media teacher to go into the collaborative teacher's classroom for research instruction. For example, moving out to classrooms is a great way to accommodate special needs students. Some ELL (English language learner) and special education classes have students who cannot handle instruction in a room the size of the library media center. They can hear, see, or concentrate better in a smaller, familiar environment. When hands-on research actually begins and students need to be shown print and electronic source locations or given technology access directions, the class will return to the LMC.

ELL/Special Modifications

Locating Sources

Quality of Sources

What is the condition of your collection? Do students have trouble finding the materials they need in your library media center? Do some teachers actually avoid using your facility because over the years they have learned they must send their classes to the public library for a better selection of current materials? Initiating collaborative research instruction is an ideal opportunity for you to appeal for funding for collection improvement. Although the three lessons of the Research Process remain essentially the same for each collaborative unit, students' topics should be based on different content-area standards which form the basis for teachers' units of study. Since the LMC collection should be updated in direct response to the resource needs of collaborative units, the library media teacher should logically become a site leader in aligning curriculum with standards.

Content-Area Standard

Variety of Sources

The Research Process reflects the need for all students to access, evaluate, read, comprehend, and use a variety of formats of information. *Sources* refers to all forms of information, while *formats* distinguishes among the kinds of sources of information such as a book, reference, or CD-ROM, or the Internet. Lesson 2 on sources is based on the concept that research means using more than one format of information. The choice of a minimum of three formats of information (see *Figure 3-5*) provides a baseline for the minimum amount of information access training needed for high school students to have adequate instruction in locational and bibliographic contextualized skills.

Technology Proficiency

Fig. 3-3. LMC Planning Map

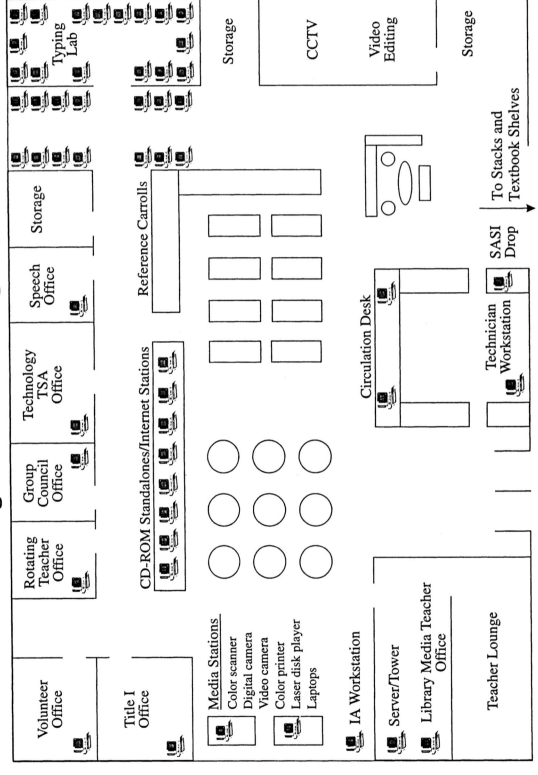

From *Practical Steps to the Research Process for High School* © 1999 Libraries Unlimited. 800-237-6124.

Do not let lack of resources restrict or deter collaborative planning and teaching. Most LMCs, no matter how deprived, can provide a bare minimum of three formats of information, always including both print and electronic choices. For example, Lesson 1, Developing a Topic, revolves around the concept that a good topic depends on the availability of information matched to the ability of the student to read and comprehend. For a variety of reasons, some students absolutely require on-campus topics, while other students are able to access and use public and college libraries. Therefore, to be able to provide adequate topic selection, the LMC collection needs a baseline variety of formats of information for the students who absolutely need them, not necessarily an enormous quantity to meet the needs of every single student.

It is easy to see why an active, instructionally involved library media center is often either a better equipped or a more well rounded facility. This becomes a mandate for educational reform: Put library media teachers in every school who can determine standards-based resources and deliver information literacy-based instruction.

Important Idea

Preparing Equipment/Technology

The power of collaborative teaching, which services the needs of the entire faculty and student body of the school site, legitimizes the need to have a technologically advanced library media center because: 1) preparing for a variety of formats so essential in Lesson 2, Looking at Sources, requires the LMC to have a technology plan in place with specific yearly hardware and software goals based on information literacy needs; 2) it is advantageous for the library media teacher to prepare a computer map of the facility (*Figure 3-3*) which is always available for technology reconfiguration as changes in funding arise; and 3) the wall calendar of scheduled research lessons vividly demonstrates to the administration that the LMC is truly in demand as a technology and information hub for the school.

Technology Proficiency

Considering the technology needs of students, equipment preparation may include the long-term selection of hardware which accommodates the baseline software and networkable information sources. When students begin hands-on research, basic technology information access would include both electronic sources such as software and CD-ROMs, as well as networkable sources such as online search tools and the Internet. The LMT should caution students to make the best use of their limited time by first using those sources of information which are only available to them at school.

When it comes to flexibility in providing research instruction, what makes setup and room switching so easy is the old reliable pull-down screen and overhead projector. This book has been formatted with templates for overhead transparencies for the three Research Process lessons. A conversion of these lessons and templates into a multimedia presentation would be a wonderful challenge. Role modeling innovative technology integration is a good reason for the library media teacher to request ongoing funding to update library media center computers and peripheral devices such as scanners and digital cameras.

Preparing for the Unit and Lessons

Content-Area Standard

Information Literacy

Unit Concepts

Preparations to begin teaching the unit are defined in the planning stage through a division of tasks between the classroom teacher and the library media teacher. First, the classroom teacher introduces the students to content-area concepts which are identified on the lesson planning sheet (*Figure 2-4*). Students need to have a definite purpose in mind when they arrive in the library media center. Second, the library media teacher teaches the information literacy concepts and strategies contextualized to individual topics to meaningfully accomplish the classroom teacher's goals for the project's research, construction, and completion.

Unit Time

Generally: Through collaborative lessons, classroom teachers gain a much better understanding of adequate hands-on research time. Often, teachers are not familiar with the steps of research and the time it takes students to successfully learn and use strategies for selecting topics and subtopics, locating and evaluating sources, reading critically, notetaking, correctly constructing bibliography entries, writing rough and final drafts, and typing and preparing a presentation. Inadvertently, a teacher's brief research timetable may have caused students to resort to some measure of plagiarism. Collaborative teaching of the Research Process changes all of that! For the first time teachers may understand that successfully learning how to accomplish the steps of research is just as important as the research product. This is what information literacy is all about: a focus on process as well as product so that students emerge from an information management experience equipped with lifelong skills.

Lifelong Skills

Specifically: The teacher determines the extent of a collaborative project. It could be merely a one-period target or supplementary lesson, or it could constitute an entire unit. A definite factor in motivating classroom teachers to spend more time in collaborative projects is the library media teacher's willingness to make time concessions. Even the quick-paced three days of research lessons may be too much for a teacher's time constraints. Adjust accordingly. Teaching a research step out of sequence does not mean it is out of context. The teacher beginning science fair projects may only have time for a bibliography lesson so that students can cite sources for topic ideas.

Compressing Research Process lecture time into three days is challenging to students. This is a lot of information not only for the instructor to deliver, but for students to absorb. High school is the only level where the library media teacher may be able to get away with three straight days of lecture without intermittent hands-on supporting activities, which is absolutely essential for elementary and middle school students. In general, the high school student is better equipped to "drink from a fire hose." They are more mature, have longer attention spans, and can digest more information. What they don't get during the three instruction days makes sense to them on the fourth day when they begin hands-on research. The timing of the three lessons offered in this book must remain flexible enough to adapt to the special needs of teachers and students. Again, adjust accordingly!

Unit Materials

Teacher materials: The collaborating teacher prepares classroom content-area materials and specific project requirements for the unit and gives copies to the library media teacher. Based on that teacher's unit needs, the LMT prepares specific information literacy instructional materials used for the research lessons. As seen in previous sections, preparation can include a wide range of materials from facility signage to hardware/software pathfinders to the templates in the student research packet. This book reflects years of creating preparation material for units which can be used as-is or modified as needed.

Content-Area Standard

LMT presentation materials: Let's face it, the teaching and learning of research strategies is not often considered dynamically, earth-shatteringly interesting to students! So how does a library media teacher accomplish the seemingly impossible? The key to creating effective information management lesson materials is relevance. Without it, learning how to write a correct bibliography entry or how to construct a good note is, frankly, tedious and boring. If students don't see meaning and purpose relevant to their immediate project, they'll simply tune out. Few will perceive the research strategies in these lessons as lifelong skills until that connection is personally meaningful. For the instructor, a measure of personality interjection—yes, even hype—may be called for!

Information Literacy

There are two important items for creating relevance. The first is humor. Many thanks are extended to the talented humorists who have granted copyright permission for the reproduction of their insightful cartoons. At strategic points, they introduce, in a poignant way, what would ordinarily be very dry and boring research concepts. The second extraordinarily important resource is the generous use of student samples. Seeing the good, and especially the bad, examples of fellow students' work provides invaluable relevance which dramatically raises the class's level of understanding.

Important Idea

Lifelong Skills

A disclaimer: Separate the content of the lessons in this guide book from the style of presentation portrayed. Remember, besides presenting the steps of research, this is a diary of one person's successful instructional strategies. The reader must adapt the content to their own personal style of delivery. But, be prepared! Despite an instructor's best efforts, there will be restlessness on the part of less mature students. It is my experience that if you have had past success with your teaching style, attribute the small percent of student problems to information overload, not necessarily to boredom. Adjust lessons accordingly. The LMT's ability to ad lib anecdotes from personal experience, with added touches of patience and perseverance, will be rewarded! By the first day of hands-on research, even the students who seemingly weren't paying attention bustle off with true purpose. Others begin to ask you incredibly intelligent questions about sources and notes. It's a miracle!

Student Handouts

Based on the concept that less is more, the research packet for high school students, seen on the following pages, represents years of research lessons distilled into four guide sheets to be given out on two consecutive days. On the first day of instruction in Lesson 1, students will receive the Research Process (*Figure 3-4*), and the Research Checklist sheets (*Figure 3-5*). On the second day of instruction in Lesson 2, they will receive the Bibliography Activity sheet (*Figure 3-6*) which is a hands-on activity created to clearly learn the Bibliography: MLA Examples sheets (*Figures 3-7* and *3-8*).

Though all of these guide sheets appear later in the book in their appropriate chapters, these handouts are also grouped on the following pages so that they may be clearly seen as the entire student packet for this series of lessons. The research packet for teachers is much more inclusive, containing overhead transparency templates as well as student handouts.

Fig. 3-4. Research Process

Topic
A. Locate topic ideas in grade-level texts, unit concepts, current literature studies.
B. Check in the library media center for sources to determine supporting information.
C. Cross-check in an encyclopedia to narrow or broaden a topic.
D. Create a thesis statement to investigate the topic.

Subtopics
A. Ask yourself: What do I want to know about my topic?
B. Specific: Pre-search encyclopedia or nonfiction book's table of contents for ideas.
C. General:
    Thing: who, what, when, where, why/how.
    Person: early life, education, accomplishments, later life.
D. Minimum of three subtopics; maximum is determined by time and information.
E. List subtopics in outline form by Roman numeral. Construct outline guide.

Sources
A. Source: Anything used for information.
    Format of sources:
        Print: books, references, magazines, newspapers, maps, charts, etc.
        Nonprint: videos, software, CD-ROMs, Internet.
B. Number of formats (minimum of three). Number of sources.
C. Credit sources using an official guide such as the MLA Bibliography sheet.
D. Know the difference:
    Primary vs. secondary sources.
    Regular vs. annotated bibliography.

Read/Think/Select
A. Read an entire "chunk" *before* selecting facts. Put your pencil down!
B. Think about what was read. What was important?
C. Select appropriate information from each "chunk."

Notetake
A. Note cards: One note per card! Title cards with subtopics.
B. Notebook Paper: Bullet or mark each note. Do not number notes at this time.
C. Record only important facts or keywords.
D. Discard small words like *a*, *an*, and *the*. Use commas and dashes instead.
E. No sentences!
F. Use quotation marks when copying. Give credit with source and page number.
G. Alternative information gathering includes paraphrasing or summarizing.

Sort and Number Notes
A. Sort notes by subtopic, by paragraph ideas, and then by supporting details (outline).
B. Read all your notes. Select good notes; discard irrelevant notes.
C. Sequence notes for fluent writing.
D. Number all notes consecutively from section to section.

Extension
    Write/Publish/Present
    Final bibliography
    Technology integration

Evaluation

From *Practical Steps to the Research Process for High School* © 1999 Libraries Unlimited. 800-237-6124.

Fig. 3-5. Research Checklist

LMT/Teacher Tracking	Points

Topic _____

Subtopics

    I. _____

    II. _____

    III. _____

    IV. _____

    V. _____

Sources

    A. At least 3 formats (book, reference, interview, CD-ROM, Internet, etc.)

    B. Total number of sources: _____

Read and notetake

    A. At least 10 notes for each subtopic.

    B. Total number of notes:_____

Sort and number notes

Write rough draft from notes

LMT/Teacher Grading

Title page

Typed report

Final bibliography

Presentation activity

From *Practical Steps to the Research Process for High School* © 1999 Libraries Unlimited. 800-237-6124.

Fig. 3-6. Bibliography Activity

Name_____ Teacher _____

Alphabetical order _____

Bibliography: Encyclopedia

Author *if available* (last name, first name, middle) _____ (period)

Article title ("quotation marks") _____ (period)

Title of encyclopedia (underlined)_____ (period)

Year_____ followed by: *ed* (period)

Example: Barnes, Isaac Jacob. "Camels." The World Book Encyclopedia. 1996 ed.

- -

Alphabetical order _____

Bibliography: CD-ROM Encyclopedia

Author *if available* (last name, first name) _____ (period)

Article Title ("quotation marks") _____ (period)

CD-ROM Title (underlined)_____ (period)

Edition (abbreviate the word edition) _____(period)

Write the words: *CD-ROM* (period)

Year_____ followed by: *ed* (period)

Example: Adams, Ernest D. "Spanish Armada." The World Book Multimedia Encyclopedia. Deluxe ed. CD-ROM. 1998 ed.

- -

Alphabetical order _____

Bibliography: Internet Web Site

Title of web site ("quotation marks") _____ (period)

Date of access: Day (numeric) Month (abbreviated) Year_____ (no period)

URL (<web site address in brackets>) _____ (period)

Example: "Watergate." 5 Oct. 1998 <http://www.cnn.com>.

From *Practical Steps to the Research Process for High School* © 1999 Libraries Unlimited. 800-237-6124.

Fig. 3-7. Bibliography: MLA Examples

Except for starred items, all examples are from the following web site:
12 Feb. 1999 <http://ollie.dcccd.edu/library/Module4/M4-V/examples.htm>.

BOOKS:

No author*
People of Long Ago. Milwaukee: Rourke Publishers, 1986.

One author*
Newberry, Louis. Hair Design. Los Angeles: Newberry Press, 1986.

Two authors
Zwerdling, Alex, and Richard Voorhees. Orwell and the Left. New Haven: Yale UP, 1974.

More than two authors*
Kingsley, Eric, et al. Ships. New York: Alfred A. Knopf, 1995.

Edited
Foster, Carol E., Mark A. Siegel, and Nancy R. Jacobs, eds. Women's Changing Role. The Information Series on Current Topics. Wylie: Information Plus, 1990.

By a corporation*
Dallas County Community College District. Richland College. Institutional Self-Study. Dallas: Richland College, 1993.

SPECIAL BOOKS:

Anthology or multi-volume set
"Fromm, Erich 1900-1980." Contemporary Authors.Vol. 29. New Revision Series. Detroit: Gale, 1990. 55 vols. to date. 1981- .

Atlas
Atlas of the World. New York: Oxford UP, 1992. Munro, David, ed.

Dictionary
"Hard Rock." The American Heritage Dictionary of the English Language. 3rd ed. Boston: Houghton, 1993.

Poem, play, or short story from an anthology
Chekhov, Anton. The Cherry Orchard. Trans. Avraham Yarmolinsky. Norton Anthology of World Masterpieces. Ed. Maynard Mack. 4th ed. Vol. 2. New York: Norton, 1979. 1192-1230. 2 vols.

ENCYCLOPEDIAS:

In print, with author
Landry, Tom. "Football." World Book Encyclopedia. 1991 ed.

In print, no author
"Industrial Architecture." New Caxton Encyclopedia. London: Caxton, 1977. 20 vols.

Fig. 3-8. Bibliography: MLA Examples

CD-ROM:
Encyclopedia article
Kumbier, William A. "Science Fiction." <u>World Book 1997 Multimedia Encyclopedia</u>. Deluxe ed. CD-ROM. 1997 ed.
Newspaper article
Birnbaum, Mary C. "Information-Age Infants: Technology Pushes the Frontiers of What Babies Know." <u>Dallas Morning News</u> 23 Aug. 1994: 5C. <u>NewsBank CD News</u>. CD-ROM.

INTERNET:
Web site
"Hank Aaron." 1996. <u>Total Baseball</u>. Tot@lSports. 6 May 1997 <http://www. totalbaseball.com>.
Encyclopedia article
Enfield, David B. "El Niño." <u>Britannica Online</u>. Vers. 98.2. Apr. 1998. Encyclopedia Britannica. 1 Jul. 1998 <http://www.eb.com>.
Magazine article
Kluger, Jeffrey. "The Gentle Cosmic Rain." <u>Time</u>. 9 Jun. 1997. 11 Jun. 1997 <http://www.pathfinder.com/index.htm>.
Newspaper article
Johnson, George. "Don't Worry: A Brain Still Can't Be Cloned. " <u>New York Times</u>. 2 Mar. 1997, forums sec. 11 Jun. 1997 <http://forums.nytimes.com/library/ national/0302clone-review.html>.
E-mail
Jeser-Skaggs, Sharlee (sjs@dcccd.edu). "Keyword Quirks." E-mail to Gary Duke (gd@dcccd.edu). 28 Feb. 1995.

MAGAZINES:
Article, with author
Idelson, Holly. "Gun Rights and Restrictions." <u>Congressional Quarterly Weekly Report</u>. 24 Apr. 1993: 1021-27.
Article, no author
"Stolen Art Treasures Found in Texas." <u>Facts on File</u>. 22 Jun. 1990: 459.

NEWSPAPERS:
Article, with author
Moreno, Sylvia. "Senate Endorses Gun Bill after Brief Filibuster." <u>Dallas Morning News</u>. 18 May 1993: 1A+.
Article, no author*
"Aiding the Arts." <u>The Milwaukee Sentinel</u>. 15 Jan. 1997: 3B

MISCELLANEOUS
Film and video
<u>The Wrong Stuff: American Architecture</u>. Videocassette. Dir. Tom Bettag. Carousel Films, 1983.
Interview
Face to face: Pei, I. M. Personal interview. 27 Jul. 1983.
Telephone: Poussaint, Alvin F. Telephone interview. 10 Dec. 1980.
Pamphlet
Treat like a book.

From *Practical Steps to the Research Process for High School* © 1999 Libraries Unlimited. 800-237-6124.

Section 2
The Research Process

Chapter 4

Developing a Topic:
Lesson 1, Part 1

Instructor

Student Lesson

"This is a topic I can really sink my teeth into. I've already found tons of information."

—Student

Fig. 4-1. Research Process: Topic

Topic
A. Locate topic ideas in grade-level texts, unit concepts, current literature studies.
B. Check in the library media center for sources to determine supporting information.
C. Cross-check in an encyclopedia to narrow or broaden a topic.
D. Create a thesis statement to investigate the topic.

Subtopics
A. Ask yourself: What do I want to know about my topic?
B. Specific: Pre-search encyclopedia or nonfiction book's table of contents for ideas.
C. General:
   Thing: who, what, when, where, why/how.
   Person: early life, education, accomplishments, later life.
D. Minimum of three subtopics; maximum is determined by time and information.
E. List subtopics in outline form by Roman numeral. Construct outline guide.

Sources
A. Source: Anything used for information.
   Format of sources:
      Print: books, references, magazines, newspapers, maps, charts, etc.
      Nonprint: videos, software, CD-ROMs, Internet.
B. Number of formats (minimum of three). Number of sources.
C. Credit sources using an official guide such as the MLA Bibliography sheet.
D. Know the difference:
   Primary vs. secondary sources.
   Regular vs. annotated bibliography.

Read/Think/Select
A. Read an entire "chunk" *before* selecting facts. Put your pencil down!
B. Think about what was read. What was important?
C. Select appropriate information from each "chunk."

Notetake
A. Note cards: One note per card! Title cards with subtopics.
B. Notebook Paper: Bullet or mark each note. Do not number notes at this time.
C. Record only important facts or keywords.
D. Discard small words like *a*, *an*, and *the*. Use commas and dashes instead.
E. No sentences!
F. Use quotation marks when copying. Give credit with source and page number.
G. Alternative information gathering includes paraphrasing or summarizing.

Sort and Number Notes
A. Sort notes by subtopic, by paragraph ideas, and then by supporting details (outline).
B. Read all your notes. Select good notes; discard irrelevant notes.
C. Sequence notes for fluent writing.
D. Number all notes consecutively from section to section.

Extension
Write/Publish/Present
Final bibliography
Technology integration

Evaluation

From *Practical Steps to the Research Process for High School* © 1999 Libraries Unlimited. 800-237-6124.

Chapter Concepts

Where Do Topics Come From?

A list provided by the teacher is the most obvious source of topics, but the purpose of the Research Process: Topic sheet (*Figure 4-1*) is student independence in topic selection. It directs the student to look in a grade-level text for appropriate topic options. Of course there are many other sources of topics to which the LMT can refer during the student lesson. Literature, library books, and encyclopedias are a few examples of alternative sources. Remind students to challenge themselves. Encourage them to choose the unfamiliar in order to learn.

What Makes a Topic Good?

The one word answer: Information. Is information about the student's topic available on campus or off, and is the student physically able to retrieve it? Is topic information appropriate to the student's age, grade level, interest level, language, and learning ability? Is it appropriately challenging? Will it provide a valuable learning experience for the unit?

Does the Topic Match the Student?

This is perhaps the most important point of the chapter. By seeking both availability and readability of information, by evaluating information to broaden or narrow the topic, to provide easy access or to challenge the student, the ultimate goal of a topic is student success! The real question students must ask themselves is, "Is the topic good for me?"

What Is the Role of the Instructor in Matching Topics to Students?

One of the important services a library media teacher can offer is to take the collaborative teacher's pre-existing topic list and align the choices with the availability of library media center sources of information, including both print and electronic sources. The goal of any project is student success. High achievers can be referred to college and public libraries. Average achievers should have topic information available on campus. Low achievers can have topics pre-selected from on-campus resources appropriate to their learning level.

Instructor Information

Preparing for the First Day's Lesson

If another class is scheduled to share the library media center during a collaborative research lesson, prearrange teaching conditions with both teachers. It is important that the self-monitoring teacher who is sharing the facility keep his or her class quiet and on task without the library media teacher's assistance. The collaborative teaching partner understands the importance of:

Time

Getting to the library media center on time is not just courteous, it's essential. Whenever possible, arrange to have the class report directly to the LMC instead of their classroom.

Housekeeping

Prearrange with the teacher to have classroom management activities, such as attendance or collecting homework, taken care of while students are being seated in the LMC. At the same time, the LMT passes out handouts for that day's research lesson.

Discipline

Introduce yourself to the students as the library media *teacher*. Remind them that the library media center is a classroom and school-wide rules apply. Funny looks on some students' faces emphasize how critically important this lesson is for establishing the role of the LMT as an instructional faculty member, not only among the teaching staff but especially among the students. Remember to prearrange special seating of students the teacher knows will be distracting.

Lifelong Skills

Important Idea

Creating "Buy-In" Through Relevance

I kick off the three days of lecture with this dichotomy: The student will learn lifelong skills with which to accomplish an immediate task. First, through cartoon humor (*Figure 4-2*) and strategic questioning, I try to get students to buy-in to the fact that Research Process strategies are lifelong skills which will help them manage information for any teacher's project in any subject in high school and college. Next, I offer them the Research Process as a recipe for success to complete the project for this particular teacher. Balancing a lifelong skills perspective against, "This paper is due in two weeks," is an interesting challenge met by the information literacy strategies of each research step.

Research Process Guide Sheet

Following an introductory discussion of the cartoon, the instructor should take a few minutes to read to the class the Research Process sheet (*Figure 4-1*). The student script does not include this portion of instruction because it is repetitive. However, an initial overview of the entire process is very important to give students a frame for what will be discussed in the three days of lessons. Explain to the students that:

- if they are absent, they will miss something extremely important that time will not permit repeating, although individual assistance is always available during the days of hands-on research.

- if they feel they "know what to do" due to previous research training, these steps may provide a new, intuitive understanding of how to approach and manage information.

Lifelong
Skills

One collaborating teacher commented, "I hate to teach research because I never really learned a good system myself." After only the first day's lesson from this series, another teacher commented, "Why wasn't I shown this in high school. It's like riding a bicycle. They'll never forget it!"

Fig. 4-2. Lifelong Skills Cartoon

"THE MARKET COLLAPSED TODAY AFTER REPORTS THAT THE GLOBAL WORK FORCE IS NOW TOO EDUCATED TO EXPLOIT."

© 1997 Joel Pett, *Phi Delta Kappan.* Reprinted by permission.

Student Lesson

Getting Started

Timing: As quickly as possible.

LMT: Welcome to the library media center. Did everyone get a research packet? Write your name at the top. I have a cartoon up here on the overhead (*Figure 4-2*). Can everyone see?

Creating "Buy-in" Through Relevance

Timing: 5 minutes.

LMT: Look at these two big-wig executives. Do you perceive an attitude? (Give students a moment to ponder.) What does exploit mean?

Student: When someone takes advantage of you.

LMT: Yes. Have you ever been to a flea market and seen 10 items for a dollar? Think about the people who made those items. They were probably only paid a few pennies. But the vendor who buys and sells the items doesn't care a thing about these people. They are exploited! Why?

Student: They probably don't know any better.

LMT: Exactly! How could that possibly relate to you?

Student: We need to get a good job, so someone doesn't walk all over us.

LMT: Exactly. You are the global work force! You are setting yourself up to be taken advantage of, yes exploited, if you don't begin now to prepare yourself with skills and strategies for the world of work you will soon enter. It's not enough to just "get through" high school. You need to take classes that are meaningful to the goals you are setting.

Student: So what good is this history class?

LMT: Great question! To answer you, I want to tell you something even more confusing. Here is a curious thing: The job you will eventually do probably does not even exist at this moment.

My job as a library media teacher certainly didn't exist when I was in high school. Of course there were books, but there were no computers, no Internet! As a matter of fact, this job did not exist until after I had been teaching for quite a while. One day my principal came up to me at a summer workshop and said, "I'd like to start a new position that has just been invented called a library media teacher. I'm not quite clear about it, but it has something to do with curriculum and technology being taught in the library. Anyway, I thought it sounded like something you'd be interested in." And here I am today!

Student: And this concerns us?

LMT: If your teachers have the curious predicament of preparing you for a world that doesn't exist, what can they teach you that has any meaning? My point is, what does this cartoon possibly have to do with why you're here today?

Student: If we don't learn, we'll all be living in houses with no bathrooms?

LMT: The solution is that we equip you with what are called "lifelong skills." These are the skills that you can use in every subject, with every teacher, every time they ask you to do a report or project that requires searching for information. Chances are, every job you do in the future will also require you to know how to go about managing information. That is why you are here! We will spend only three class periods walking you step-by-step through some basic information management strategies. It's a lot to show you in a short period of time, but,

"How do you eat an elephant?"
"One bite at a time."

Topic Strategies

Timing: 20 minutes.

LMT: Please refer to the Research Process sheet (*Figure 4-1*) in your student packet. I will break research down into such digestible bites that for the rest of your life you'll say to your teacher, "I know how to do that!" Even better news for you today is, at the same time that you are truly equipping yourself for the future, you will be accomplishing exactly what your teacher wants you to do in the next couple of weeks: create a research project about your topic. Let's start with this basic question, "Where do topics come from?"

Important Idea

**Problem
Solving**

**Content-Area
Standard**

Student: Our teacher gave us a list and told us to pick.

LMT: You're lucky this time. You know, as you move on through high school, and especially as you go on into junior or regular college, your teacher may just tell you, "Your topic is due in two days." That's as helpful as it gets. So what can you do, on your own, to pick out a good topic? This raises another important question, "What makes a topic *good*?"

Student: Something you'd like to know about, not boring.

LMT: Great point! If you hate it, you'll be less likely to want to find out about it. Sometimes, however, you think you hate something just because you don't know anything about it. I encourage you to tackle those tough, unknown topics you can really learn about! For most of us, liking it is not really the way we judge whether it's a good topic. Any more ideas?

Student: Whether I can find anything about it.

LMT: Now you've got it! The key to whether a topic is good is *information*! Let's take a minute to figure out where topics come from, so we can begin to judge whether it's a good one for us. Letter A on your guide sheet says, "Locate topic ideas in grade-level texts." Does it make sense that an easy way to come up with a topic is simply to open up the textbook? It could be the history, science, or literature book your class is reading. If something there catches your attention, it *must* be appropriate: It's at your grade level; it's the unit your teacher is studying; it caught your interest. Perfect, right?

Fig. 4-3. Narrow or Broaden a Topic

Pre-search your topic to see if there is *too much* information.
Then select a subtopic to become your topic.
This might happen several times.

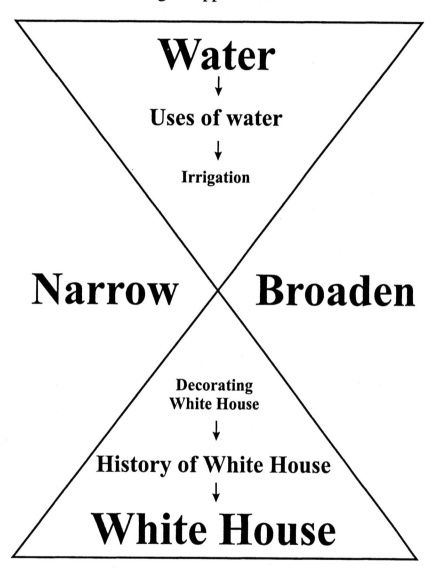

Pre-search your topic to see if there is *not enough* information.
You will probably see that it is the subtopic of a larger topic.
This might happen several times.

From *Practical Steps to the Research Process for High School* © 1999 Libraries Unlimited. 800-237-6124.

LMT: Now look at letter B on your Research Process sheet. It says, "Check in the library media center for sources to determine supporting information." Has this happened to you? You get to the library media center, and guess what? There's almost nothing there... except the Internet, perhaps. But you will see in tomorrow's lesson on sources, that's not enough!

The point is, while you're in high school, your teachers care just as much about *how* you do something as *what* you do. What is the strategy we've been identifying in this discussion?

Student: Picking a topic based on information.

Student: Does that mean just do what's easy?

Literacy

LMT: One answer is yes, you do pick a topic based on information availability, if you consider that "easy." Another answer is no, you're supposed to challenge yourself, stretch yourself to learn. If you have the time, the transportation, and the reading ability to visit local college and public libraries, then pick a topic that demands that input. But I also know that some of you work after school, or you don't have a car, so a public library is sometimes not an option.

There is another important way to help you choose a topic that's right for you. Letter C says, "Cross-check in an encyclopedia to narrow or broaden a topic." Let's look at this example (*Figure 4-3*). If your topic is buried as a minor sub-heading in an encyclopedia, such as this small section on decorating the White House. (*LMT may show an example of an encyclopedia sub-sub-heading.*) That's a hint it may be hard to find in other sources as well. This student may have to expand, or broaden, the topic to "History of the White House," or even "White House," depending on what information is available.

Problem Solving

On the other hand, if a topic has multiple sub-sections in an encyclopedia, you may want to narrow, or focus, on one of the smaller sections. For example, water is an enormous topic, so one of the subtopics or smaller sub-sections, such as "Irrigation," could easily become the topic. The decision to broaden or narrow a topic is something only you can make a judgment about.

In conclusion, deciding what is a good topic means deciding what is a good topic for *you*. Do you need to find everything here on campus? Are you able to get to the public library? Are you struggling in high school and need something relatively easy? Are you planning on a four-year college and need to really challenge yourself? Only you know these answers, and therefore only you can pick your best topic. Your teacher and I are here to both assist and challenge you. Successful topic selection is your first step in how to manage information.

Chapter 5

Developing Subtopics:
Lesson 1, Part 2

Instructor

Student Lesson

"Oh, I get it. Now I know what to look for!"

—Student

Fig. 5-1. Research Process: Subtopics

Topic
A. Locate topic ideas in grade-level texts, unit concepts, current literature studies.
B. Check in the library media center for sources to determine supporting information.
C. Cross-check in an encyclopedia to narrow or broaden a topic.
D. Create a thesis statement to investigate the topic.

Subtopics
A. Ask yourself: What do I want to know about my topic?
B. Specific: Pre-search encyclopedia or nonfiction book's table of contents for ideas.
C. General:
    Thing: who, what, when, where, why/how.
    Person: early life, education, accomplishments, later life.
D. Minimum of three subtopics; maximum is determined by time and information.
E. List subtopics in outline form by Roman numeral. Construct outline guide.

Sources
A. Source: Anything used for information.
    Format of sources:
        Print: books, references, magazines, newspapers, maps, charts, etc.
        Nonprint: videos, software, CD-ROMs, Internet.
B. Number of formats (minimum of three). Number of sources.
C. Credit sources using an official guide such as the MLA Bibliography sheet.
D. Know the difference:
    Primary vs. secondary sources.
    Regular vs. annotated bibliography.

Read/Think/Select
A. Read an entire "chunk" *before* selecting facts. Put your pencil down!
B. Think about what was read. What was important?
C. Select appropriate information from each "chunk."

Notetake
A. Note cards: One note per card! Title cards with subtopics.
B. Notebook Paper: Bullet or mark each note. Do not number notes at this time.
C. Record only important facts or keywords.
D. Discard small words like *a*, *an*, and *the*. Use commas and dashes instead.
E. No sentences!
F. Use quotation marks when copying. Give credit with source and page number.
G. Alternative information gathering includes paraphrasing or summarizing.

Sort and Number Notes
A. Sort notes by subtopic, by paragraph ideas, and then by supporting details (outline).
B. Read all your notes. Select good notes; discard irrelevant notes.
C. Sequence notes for fluent writing.
D. Number all notes consecutively from section to section.

Extension
    Write/Publish/Present
    Final bibliography
    Technology integration

Evaluation

From *Practical Steps to the Research Process for High School* © 1999 Libraries Unlimited. 800-237-6124.

Chapter Concepts

Why Subtopics Are Essential

"If you don't have subtopics, you have no idea what you're doing!" is the statement you'll see in the student lesson script. This concept cannot be too strongly stressed. Subtopics are the frame, the filter, the guide, the evaluative criteria for the information search. They tell the student what to look for in every source and, just as important, what to skip. This is the most tangible of the information management skills. When will students copy directly from a source? When information is of no greater or lesser value. With subtopics as identifying tools, the information in all formats and sources is practically self-sorting!

What Do You Want to Know?

It is essential that students "pre-search" before they "re-search." Pre-searching is a cursory, evaluative step that is mandatory to determine if there is enough available, readable material to warrant searching again (re-searching), for information.

Finding Subtopics

Subtopics are not invented. They can be derived, for example, from the subtopics already available in encyclopedias or the table of contents of books about the topic. The number of subtopics is a key factor in matching the topic to the student. Time for hands-on research is a critical factor for the LMT and collaborating teacher in setting the number of subtopics which can be accomplished *successfully* by average students.

Modifying Research for Special Students

Advanced students have more subtopics; special needs students have fewer. In this way, the literacy and learning needs of all students are met in a simple and highly appropriate way. The success of every student as measured by improved achievement is real.

 # Instructor Information

This Will Change Your Life!

Identifying subtopics as a strategy for gathering information seems to be the "missing link" of general research. To establish a link to prior knowledge, remind students that subtopics appear in outlining, a technique they should be very familiar with. Classroom teachers are good at teaching students to outline information *from* a

Important Idea

text or source, but they do not translate this technique to outlining for information not yet gathered. An outline is usually thought of as "after the fact." With the Research Process, subtopics become the guide to gathering, as well as analyzing, information. This point cannot be emphasized enough!

Problem

How can students develop subtopics for unknown information?

Solution

They are not expected to! As a homework assignment for the first and second days' lessons, send students to the LMC to do preliminary searching, called "pre-searching," for subtopics, as explained in the student script. Locating the bold-face sub-headings in encyclopedias or the chapter titles in the table of contents of nonfiction books are strategies for creating subtopics. They become the "bare bones" which are "fleshed out" with notetaking. With subtopics, suddenly the project is not nearly as threatening. This strategy of information management enables students to begin to see clearly what they're supposed to do. The increase in efficient, on-task use of hands-on research time in the library media center is a remarkable sight to see!

Factors That Determine Subtopics

What form does a subtopic take? As recorded on the Research Checklist (*Figure 5-2*), subtopics are the keywords taken from the essential questions the student wants the research to answer. Simple subtopics such as *what, who, when, where, why,* and *how* become the roots for flexible guide questions to locate information. This hits at the nature of research. It is problem solving. Subtopics should answer the following questions.

- What information do I *access* about my topic?
- What information helps me *evaluate* my topic?
- How do I creatively *use* my topic?

Content-Area Standard

Literacy

Pre-Search Before Re-Search

The Key to Appropriate Topics

Teacher's have enough to do! Wouldn't they be happy if the students themselves had a strategy for locating appropriate unit (standards-based) topics? "Appropriate" means topics that have enough readable and available information in a variety of sources on campus. "Enough" information means the topic can be broken down into information-rich subtopics. Subtopics determine whether there is enough appropriate information to pursue a topic meaningfully.

I'll never forget the year I gave "Space Medicine" as the topic for a health term paper to a sixth grader! Did I bother to go to our little school library to see if that topic had supporting information? No one ever told me I should do that! Meanwhile, this poor student's exasperated parents spent many nights in the local college library trying, with great difficulty, to access information in periodicals and such. This child could barely read his sixth-grade text, much less manage college-level information. You can guess who really did that project.

This was a completely irresponsible act on my part as a teacher. I did not do my homework to properly prepare a topic list and then match information availability to student ability. But then, there were no library media teachers at that time!

The Key to Narrowing or Broadening Topics

When subtopics are used to identify the availability of readable information, it is obvious when there is too much or too little. A beloved topic which has only a few paragraphs of supporting information should become the subtopic of a larger concept. The subtopic should become the topic when information is obviously too abundant. Students pre-search with subtopics to determine whether a topic should be narrowed or broadened. It is a critical thinking decision only they can make.

Problem Solving

The Key to Determining Availability of Topics.

On that first night or two when students go off to pre-search for subtopics, they run into the first real hurdle of whether or not information is available on campus. Some may come back to the teacher the next day asking to change their topics. Allow that to happen; that's the point!

Fig. 5-2. Research Checklist

LMT/Teacher Tracking	Points
Topic ____Solar car____	
Subtopics	

I. ___What is a (solar cell)?___

II. ___What is (solar energy)?___

III. ___What is (photovoltaic) ?___

IV. _____

V. _____

Sources

    A. At least 3 formats (book, reference, interview, CD-ROM, Internet, etc.)

    B. Total number of sources: _____

Read and notetake

    A. At least 10 notes for each subtopic.

    B. Total number of notes: _____

Sort and number notes

Write rough draft from notes

LMT/Teacher Grading

Title page

Typed report

Final bibliography

Presentation activity

From *Practical Steps to the Research Process for High School* © 1999 Libraries Unlimited. 800-237-6124.

ELL/Special Modifications

Through the collaborative planning process, the library media teacher takes the classroom teacher's preliminary topic list and does a general search of LMC sources. Tightening up the teacher's topic list empowers students for success in research. A few days before research lessons, give the teacher a list of topics ranked "easy" to "difficult" according to information availability. LMTs pre-search with subtopics to determine whether information validates topics.

The Research Checklist

The Research Checklist sheet (*Figure 5-2*) is a template created so that students have clear expectations about each step of the research project. It's not a "gotcha" for the teacher. This sheet empowers students!

Important Idea

A research project appears to be a teacher-invented, teacher-required, teacher-controlled, teacher-graded activity. The tracking sheet is an indicator that the whole purpose of these three days of lessons is to give control of information back to the student! It is their topic, their choice of subtopics, their choice of sources, and their ability to comprehend reading and select their choice of facts that goes into their creation of a great project.

At the end of each day's lesson, students record their selection of project information as indicated, which must align with what is expected they will accomplish for each of the Research Process steps. This guide sheet works equally well for both the student and the teacher. These are the directions I cover in the student lesson script:

Topic Expectations

• Students record their topic, if known, on the top line.

• Students may want to write in pencil.

• Students may change their topic idea until the end of the first day of research.

• Students are matched to the level of difficulty of a topic through teacher approval.

Subtopic Expectations

Information Literacy

• Subtopics can be either generic or specific. Novice researchers will want to pre-search for specific subtopics. They need the concrete experience of spending time in the LMC searching for sources of information to validate a topic before research can occur. They need to locate subtopic ideas by using specific strategies such as checking the sub-headings in encyclopedias and chapter titles in a book's table of contents. The presence of subtopics in sources means supporting information exists! For more experienced students, generic subtopics (*Figure 5-1*) are less concrete and often require more abstract analysis of information, yet they work quite well for some topics.

• I require that all students, prepared or not, record at least the generic subtopics onto the Research Checklist during this part of the lesson, so they understand that this step cannot be skipped.

Strategies for Developing Subtopics

As will be seen in the student lesson script, I intentionally use hyperbole because I cannot overemphasize to students how strongly I feel about the use of subtopics as a strategy for managing information:

Important Idea

"For this project, or any research project you ever do for any teacher or any subject for the rest of your life, you cannot continue on in your research until you have recorded subtopics. Subtopics are the keywords to the essential questions about your topic which your research will answer and thereby give you the control strategies for managing information."

• Subtopics are flexible! "Whose paper is this?" I ask the class. They understand that they control information by selecting, adding, changing, combining, or eliminating subtopics.

• Subtopics should be recorded in pencil to indicate, almost symbolically, that students have control over their information.

• The minimum number of subtopics is set by the teacher, but the student can choose to exceed that number.

Research Checklist Instructions

Due Dates

Information Literacy

Content-Area Standard

The teacher's project syllabus usually sets dates for students to complete the parts of the final product. This is always different from the due dates for the steps of research on the Research Checklist, which is actually a tracking of the information management process. This concept of creating a reasonable but definite timetable and tracking each research step is critical to student success. Though the lessons on accessing sources and using them for notetaking have not yet occurred, during Lesson 1 on this first day of instruction, I can announce to students the exact number of sources and notes that are expected (by the average student) because it is based on the number of research days the teacher can allow. (Look ahead to the pacing guidelines in Chapter 11, *Figure 11-3*, p. 172.) When given small steps that are readily accomplished, students not only achieve my goal of learning the information literacy curriculum, they also have greater success in completing the final product for the teacher and therefore learning the content-area curriculum.

Looking Ahead to Accountability

Student accountability for developing those critical subtopics appears not only on the Research Checklist but is also a component of the tracking sheet developed by the LMT and collaborating teacher during the initial planning stage. A carefully tailored tool makes it easy to track each student for each step of research while yielding accurate data to augment the teacher's grading criteria. In looking ahead to the Research Tracking Sheet in Chapter 11 (*Figure 11-4*, p. 174), the number of subtopics can be exactly recorded: 3 for Jane Xxx, 2 for Susie Yyy who is in special education, and 5 for John Zzz who is in the G.A.T.E. (Gifted and Talented Education) program. Some teachers prefer a simpler plus, check mark, or minus sign. Whatever the method, it's the tracking that's important! I know from experience that it is amazing how the quantity (and quality) of work increases when students are tracked in exact amounts.

Still rooted in the product required for their own content area, some teachers choose not to track the Research Process at all. When this arises during collaborative planning, I often ask that teacher if I can track student research anyway, simply as a way of monitoring the progress of information literacy. Once the teacher sees the difference it makes in student outcome, I often win another convert to the focus on the process of information management!

Fig. 5-3. Subtopic Story

To best illustrate the importance of subtopics, I tell this dinosaur story.

Several years ago, when I was a library media teacher in an elementary school, a little boy came walking into the library media center and said, "I have to write a report about dinosaurs."

Do you have any idea how big that topic is? HUGE! Do you know how many kinds of dinosaurs there are? How many millions of years they lived on this planet?

I didn't want to tell the little boy we could be here for the next 20 years, so I asked him, "But what do you want to know about dinosaurs?" (Refer to letter A on the Research Process sheet, *Figure 5-1*.)

What I was really asking him to do was identify subtopics, so I said, "Maybe you'd like to know what a dinosaur looked like—it's body?"

"Yes!" he said, "I sure would!"

"Maybe you'd like to know what food it eats?"

"Of course. I do need to know that," he said.

"How about where it lives—its habitat?"

"Oh man, yeah. My teacher said to include that too."

"Can you think of anything else you'd be interested to know about your dinosaur? What its babies were like, or its enemies?"

By this time a light bulb had gone off in the little boy's head. He realized that he had five things to look for about dinosaurs. When he opened a book he said, "Hey, here's something about its food!" And he took "food" notes. He opened an encyclopedia and said, "Wow, here's some information about where it lives." And he took "habitat" notes. He continued, looking on a CD-ROM, and he took notes on "body," "enemies," and "babies."

The same is true in high school. If you do not select subtopics, you have no idea what you are doing in the library! You will be confused, frustrated, and will likely end up copying a lot of stuff from books or printouts.

Once you have subtopics, you know how to manage information. By titling your notebook page notes or notecards with a subtopic, you instantly pre-sort everything you find. Best of all, you know what you are looking for, and you know what to skip! This enables you to manage time as well as information.

Student Lesson

Timing: 25 minutes.

This Will Change Your Life!

LMT: This half of the lesson will change your life! (I usually get funny stares, but it gets their attention.) You may not have made a final decision on your topic, but we are still able to move on to the next step of the Research Process. Put your Research Process sheet (*Figure 5-1*) back in front of you and look at the section called "Subtopics." Believe it or not, locating your topic is *not* the most important thing in getting started on your research!

Student: How can I start if I don't know what I'm doing?

LMT: I want you to begin to understand that no matter what your topic is, you need to develop strategies to look for information. Once you learn these strategies, you can apply them to whatever topic you pick for this project and to every other project any teacher asks you to do. You will be shown specific ways to manage information each day, but this is probably the most important, so please ask questions when you are confused. Other people probably need clarification, too. For whatever topic you pick, you will always ask yourself the question, by letter A on your guide sheet:

Information Literacy

"What do I want to know about my topic?"

Factors That Determine Subtopics

LMT: The answer to this question will be your subtopics, the keys to unlocking the doors of information. Look at letter C on your sheet. If your topic is a *thing*, you could ask these questions:

Lifelong Skills

- *What* is it? Describe or define your topic for the reader.
- *Who* created, invented, or was involved with it?
- *When* did it happen (era, year, day, etc.)?
- *Where* did it happen (region, country, city, etc.)?
- *Why* and *how* did it happen?

Problem Solving

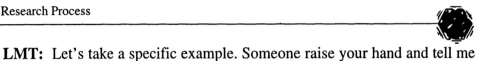

Content-Area
Standard

LMT: Let's take a specific example. Someone raise your hand and tell me the World War II topic you have chosen.

Student: I think I'm going to do the Warsaw Ghetto.

LMT: Great. Because the Warsaw Ghetto is a thing, let's apply the "General" subtopics listed on the guide sheet. Pretend I've never heard of this topic and we'll create search questions.

- What is the Warsaw Ghetto?
- Who created it? Who was in it? Who was for it, against it, etc.?
- When did it begin and end? How does this fit into the whole war scenario, and what's the significance of the time frame?
- Where was it located, and why was it located there?
- Why and how was it started, and how did it end?

Student: Yeah, I can see that works. This tells me what I need to look for.

LMT: Exacatly. Let me interject this question to everyone: "Why do kids copy from sources?"

Student: It's easy.

Student: It's quick.

Student: I put down everything that looks good to me.

Important
Idea

LMT: Yes! That's an important point. *Everything* looks good to you, so you begin to copy. In other words, without subtopics, you have no way to pick and choose information. I'm convinced that, besides the good reasons you just mentioned, kids copy because they're either overwhelmed or confused! Subtopics eliminate confusion by allowing you to identify exactly the information you have said is important about your topic.

These days, with so much information available, the best news is that subtopics also tell you what is *not* important to your topic! When you encounter information that is *not* one of your subtopics, guess what you get to do?

Student: Skip it!

Information
Literacy

LMT: Life's starting to look a little less bleak. Isn't this project getting a more manageable already? Do you see that subtopics are the critical way to begin managing information? Let's try another example. There's a second group of general subtopics listed under C on your guide sheet. Has anyone chosen a person as your World War II topic?

Student: Yes. I've picked Winston Churchill.

LMT: Good. This an easy topic in the sense that there is a tremendous amount of information available in every kind of source. There is an important thing subtopics will do for you. Subtopics will help you narrow and weed out too many facts. Also, use a source's subtopic to help you confine your subtopics for Churchill only to the World War II era. This brings up an important point for everyone, and can be applied to any other research project you're doing: Stick to your teacher's unit! Does it make sense that subtopics help focus information to the time period or unit concepts required by the teacher?

For the war years, you would probably focus entirely on subtopics specifying the accomplishments of the person's life during World War II. In other words, what did Winston Churchill do during the war years that was of significance?

ELL/Special
Modifications

Student: How do I know that? I haven't even started studying him yet?

LMT: Right! You don't know. When subtopics need to be specific, you obviously can't make them up in your head. Neither can you just say, "Accomplishments," as seen on the Research Process sheet. You do what's called "pre-search." That means you come to the LMC and find a good general source, such as an encyclopedia, as it says in letter B, and locate five specific accomplishments or actions which this person performed during World War II. For example, this encyclopedia I'm holding has "The bombing of London" in bold-face letters as a sub-heading for Churchill. That could become one of your choices for a subtopic, and likely, information about that event would be found in all the other sources as well.

Important
Idea

The general subtopics listed on the guide sheet for a person only apply when you are studying someone's complete life. Your language arts teacher, for example, may require an author report.

If, like Churchill, there is an enormous amount of information and your project is short, one of the subtopics could actually become the entire topic. Or if there is very little information on someone, like Robert Smalls during the Civil War, he may need to become a subtopic and you'd include several other notable freed slaves also as subtopics to meet your project requirements. The point is, subtopics can make quite a difference in broadening, narrowing, or validating a topic.

Problem
Solving

Let's move on to letter D on your guide sheet which says, "Minimum of 3 subtopics; maximum is determined by time and information." When I planned the unit with your teacher, based on the amount of time you will be given for research, we decided that to cover a topic thoroughly and successfully, you need at least five subtopics. We're therefore giving you five days of research here in the library media center.

**Important
Idea**

The number of subtopics is an important strategy directly related to time spent on a unit. From experience, I encourage teachers to base the number of subtopics on how many days the class can come to the library to do research after *the initial three days of lessons are finished. For five subtopics, five days of research is completely reasonable. Students who work quickly can increase the number of subtopics. Students who work slowly, or are absent, will have to work independently.*

**ELL/Special
Modifications**

Student: This is starting to make a lot of sense.

Student: I feel like I'll know what to do when we start research.

Student: Sounds good to me. I just want to get this over with.

LMT: You and your teacher know you best. Subtopics are the strategies which show the availability of information, but you also need to be challenged. This is an important part of determining the topic that is best for you. I have worked with your teacher ahead of time to develop ideas for topics which are easier, meaning enough subtopics are available here on campus, or more difficult, meaning the information will be much harder to locate, and you may even need to go to another library. This is why your teacher has final approval for your topic.

LMT: Some of you who are high achievers should definitely challenge yourselves. You are not intimidated by having to really dig for subtopics for a more difficult topic. Where will you go? When you can't follow the general subtopics listed on the Research Process guide sheet, where are other good places to go for subtopics?

Student: (Blank stares. No guesses.)

LMT: I just happen to have here a biography about Winston Churchill. As we open up the book to the table of contents and I read you some chapter titles (LMT reads), you will see that the chapters themselves can sometimes be either a direct source of subtopics, or an indirect source of ideas for creating your own subtopics.

Let's quickly review the strategies we have been identifying. For a unit like World War II with both easy and difficult topics, we don't expect you to sit here and think up subtopics out of your head. Come spend just a few minutes of your spare time in the LMC. Check first in an encyclopedia for those bold sub-headings. If that doesn't work, try looking at books about your topic, and scan chapter titles or main areas of information for those significant items which answer the question... (LMT waits expectantly.)

Whole class: What do I want to know about my topic?

LMT: Just a quick reminder about what is perhaps the most helpful strategy of all. Subtopics tell you exactly what information to read and write notes about, but more importantly, they identify what to leave out! For this person (pointing to the student) who finds far too much information when she goes to study Winston Churchill, well chosen subtopics will allow her to skip over vast amounts of data which she simply doesn't need.

Another reminder: If you find one of your original subtopics doesn't work, combine it with another one, or toss it out completely and insert a better one! Manipulating subtopics allows you to use both time and information to your best advantage.

To wind things up, do you remember what we talked about that makes a topic good?

Student: A good topic is one with enough information about it.

LMT: Yes. Does anyone see the comparison with subtopics?

Student: They tell you if there's enough information about the parts of your topic.

LMT: Very good! In other words, well chosen subtopics allow you to create a balanced research paper with equal sections. Let me emphasize this point. When I confront students about copying research papers out of a book, a lot of times they'll say, "My teacher never knows the difference." I'm here to tell you that subtopics make it incredibly easy for your teacher to tell the difference!

Your subtopics become the outline for your paper, telling not only what information to gather, but in what order the information will appear. Students who copy don't have a sense of balanced or sequential sections of a research paper. Copied information is often very narrow in scope. From the subtopics recorded on your Research Checklist, your teacher can simply check off the sections as he reads through your paper. Believe me, it makes reading and grading your paper a lot quicker, but still thorough. Subtopics make life easy for your teacher as well as for you.

It's decision time. On the Research Checklist (*Figure 5-2*), you have already recorded your topic at the top. Now take a few minutes and record what you think may be subtopics. Those of you who have a "thing" as a topic such as the Holocaust, the Nuhremburg Trials, or the SS, for today use the "General" subtopics on your Research Process sheet. Simply write: who, what, where, when, why/how. Those of you who have chosen a person, or a more difficult topic, you cannot write anything until you come in and pre-search for information. Remember to come check in a general reference first, such as an encyclopedia.

Information Literacy

Lifelong Skills

Important Idea

Student: So why do I have to dig around in all these other places if there's already enough stuff in one encyclopedia?

LMT: Excellent question. This leads us right to tomorrow's lesson on sources. We'll talk about why a report cannot come from only one source. Don't be absent! We'll cover some extremely important strategies for managing information.

Chapter 6

Looking at Sources:
Lesson 2

Instructor

Student Lesson

"Kids type their name on the top of an internet printout and turn it in as their work!"

—Frustrated teacher

Fig. 6-1. Research Process: Sources

Topic
    A.   Locate topic ideas in grade-level texts, unit concepts, current literature studies.
    B.   Check in the library media center for sources to determine supporting information.
    C.   Cross-check in an encyclopedia to narrow or broaden a topic.
    D.   Create a thesis statement to investigate the topic.

Subtopics
    A.   Ask yourself: What do I want to know about my topic?
    B.   Specific: Pre-search encyclopedia or nonfiction book's table of contents for ideas.
    C.   General:
            Thing: who, what, when, where, why/how.
            Person: early life, education, accomplishments, later life.
    D.   Minimum of three subtopics; maximum is determined by time and information.
    E.   List subtopics in outline form by Roman numeral. Construct outline guide.

Sources
    A.   Source: Anything used for information.
            Format of sources:
                Print: books, references, magazines, newspapers, maps, charts, etc.
                Nonprint: videos, software, CD-ROMs, Internet.
    B.   Number of formats (minimum of three). Number of sources.
    C.   Credit sources using an official guide such as the MLA Bibliography sheet.
    D.   Know the difference:
            Primary vs. secondary sources.
            Regular vs. annotated bibliography.

Read/Think/Select
    A.   Read an entire "chunk" *before* selecting facts. Put your pencil down!
    B.   Think about what was read. What was important?
    C.   Select appropriate information from each "chunk."

Notetake
    A.   Note cards: One note per card! Title cards with subtopics.
    B.   Notebook Paper: Bullet or mark each note. Do not number notes at this time.
    C.   Record only important facts or keywords.
    D.   Discard small words like *a*, *an*, and *the*. Use commas and dashes instead.
    E.   No sentences!
    F.   Use quotation marks when copying. Give credit with source and page number.
    G.   Alternative information gathering includes paraphrasing or summarizing.

Sort and Number Notes
    A.   Sort notes by subtopic, by paragraph ideas, and then by supporting details (outline).
    B.   Read all your notes. Select good notes; discard irrelevant notes.
    C.   Sequence notes for fluent writing.
    D.   Number all notes consecutively from section to section.

Extension
            Write/Publish/Present
            Final bibliography
            Technology integration

Evaluation

From *Practical Steps to the Research Process for High School* © 1999 Libraries Unlimited. 800-237-6124.

Chapter Concepts

Formats and Sources

A source is any kind of information accessed and used for ideas and information. Sources are generally referred to as either print or nonprint (electronic). Formats are the "kinds" of sources such as books, newspapers, CD-ROMs, or the Internet. Information literacy mandates that students use a variety of formats of information to prepare them with lifelong skills for information management.

Source Requirements

This guide book proposes that if a teacher allows three days of research, then three sources, preferably using three different formats, can reasonably be accessed through specific subtopics, read, and processed into a minimum of 10 notes per day. The availability of readable information matched to the student's ability level is factored in.

Research Can Never Be Based on a Single Source

A writing assignment using only one source is called a summary, not research. The project goal is always clarified with the collaborative teacher. If a research project is the goal, then the assumption is accessing, evaluating, and using information from *more than one* source (format) of information.

The Bibliography

The legal conditions under which information can and cannot be used are critical to information management and use. Not just crediting sources, but crediting them correctly using MLA or APA style is emphasized. Appropriate to this lesson is the LMT role of urging teachers throughout the school, and even the district, to standardize a legitimate bibliography form for a wide variety of print and nonprint formats so that students do not become confused by different teachers requiring different bibliography styles.

Fig. 6-2. Research Checklist

LMT/Teacher Tracking	Points
Topic _____	
Subtopics	

     I. _____

    II. _____

   III. _____

   IV. _____

    V. _____

Sources

    A. At least 3 formats (book, reference, interview, CD-ROM, Internet, etc.)

    B. Total number of sources: _____

Read and notetake

    A. At least 10 notes for each subtopic.

    B. Total number of notes:_____

Sort and number notes

Write rough draft from notes

LMT/Teacher Grading

Title page

Typed report

Final bibliography

Presentation activity

From *Practical Steps to the Research Process for High School* © 1999 Libraries Unlimited. 800-237-6124.

 **Instructor Information**

Formats and Sources

Information Literacy

The Problem

Do teachers know the difference between sources of information and formats of information? Is this even important? Usually "No" and an emphatic "Yes" are the answers to these two questions. Even you, as a library media teacher, may not have cognizantly emphasized the difference to your students and teachers, but I'll bet you've been teaching it all along! For example, you've probably been sending students to books, then to the Internet.

Information literacy requires students to access, evaluate, and use several formats, not just several sources, of information. Five sources for a project, for example, cannot mean five books, or five Internet web sites. No matter how many words are changed, it is plagiarism for a research project to come from only one source. An assignment from one source is called a summary and it is a completely different type of legitimate writing activity that a teacher may assign to students.

The Solution

Through the Research Process, the library media teacher easily distinguishes between sources and formats (*Figure 6-1*). Students clearly understand that five sources on the Student Checklist (*Figure 6-2*) means a combination of at least three formats—perhaps two books, one encyclopedia, and two Internet web sites. This distinction sheds a whole new light on information gathering:

- Students realize there is a greater variety of subtopic information available in the different print and nonprint formats. The result is a variety of reading opportunities, more reading comprehension, and therefore a more *literate* student.

- Students understand that different print and nonprint formats require different information accessing strategies. The result is a more *information literate* student.

- Students pace themselves more effectively by having a clear understanding of where they need to look for information. The result is a more *time efficient* student.

- Students move with greater interest from books, to CD-ROMs, to the Internet. The result is a more *motivated* student.

Copyright: Keeping Up with Giving Credit

The Problem

In my experience collaborating with teachers, knowledge of current copyright regulations for print and nonprint sources is not always high on their list of priorities. This is not purposeful; they may not have access to a source of current information, and they are already overwhelmed with their own agenda of curricular demands and student responsibilities. I am convinced teachers do not intend to be negligent in role modeling responsible use of resources as evidenced by the fact that most teachers require a bibliography as part of a research project. What is curious is:

- Teachers often do not use a correct or consistent bibliography style, such as MLA or APA.

- Grade-level and department teaching groups have rarely met to compare, much less standardize, bibliography requirements.

- Students at the same school site graduate with conflicting impressions of bibliography requirements because different teachers assign a bibliography differently.

The Solution

Important Idea

Though the widespread use of information networking mandates every teacher's personal responsibility for teaching and preserving copyright, a strategic role of the library media teacher still includes the dissemination of current copyright information. In focusing attention on information literacy as a school-wide goal, the issue of the use of copyrighted materials for students and teachers becomes paramount. It simply cannot be overemphasized.

What are some strategies for facilitating copyright issues?

- Every year the library media teacher can volunteer a back-to-school orientation, perhaps at that first faculty meeting, on current copyright issues for all teachers. Catch everyone before projects are assigned.

- The LMT can chair a committee to standardize bibliography format at the school site or at the district level, to articulate middle school to high school to local college requirements.

- The LMT can use the Internet as a source of current print and electronic copyright and bibliography guidelines, as seen in this book.

Bibliography

What Is MLA?

MLA stands for Modern Language Association. It is a "not-for-profit membership organization that promotes the study and teaching of language and literature."[1] It has numerous branches and subgroups. It is well known for its language style guide *The MLA Handbook for Writers of Research Papers*, fourth edition, by Joseph Gibaldi.

Many MLA online guidelines compiled by various educational institutions can be accessed by typing into an Internet search engine the three letters "MLA" or by typing the full name. The variations seen in different online versions are the source of the disclaimer for the version which appears in this manual. The goal is MLA-based consistency and accuracy written in a form that is easy for students to comprehend and use.

What Is APA?

"The American Psychological Association (APA), in Washington, D.C., is the largest scientific and professional organization representing psychology in the United States and is the world's largest association of psychologists. APA's membership includes more than 155,000 researchers, educators, clinicians, consultants, and students. Through its divisions in 50 subfields of psychology and affiliations with 59 state, territorial, and Canadian provincial associations, APA works to advance psychology as a science, as a profession, and as a means of promoting human welfare."[2]

In addition to the promotion of its publications directly related to psychology, the APA is known among educators for its style manuals for the writing of research and term papers, *Mastering APA Style: Instructors' Resource Guide* by Harold Gelfand and Charles J. Walker and *Publication Manual* of the APA.

In the same manner as MLA guidelines, abbreviated style guidelines for these APA publications can be accessed on the Internet.

Fig. 6-3. Copyright Cartoon

"We're working on composition today. Tomorrow we'll deal with copyright infringement."

Reprinted by permission of Charles Almon.

Student Lesson

Timing: 45 to 50 minutes.

What Is Copyright?

LMT: Hello class. Welcome to day two. I'm glad you reported straight to the LMC and were seated so quickly because we have a lot to cover today. As you were coming in, you received three new handouts for today: two called Bibliography: MLA Examples (*Figures 6-4, 6-5*) and one Bibliography Activity page (*Figure 6-6*). Set those aside for the moment, however, and take out your student packet from yesterday. Look at the Research Process sheet at the section called "Sources" (*Figure 6-1*). Stacked in the middle of your tables are encyclopedias which we will be using shortly.

To get started, look up at the cartoon on the overhead (*Figure 6-3*). This is what we are here to talk about today. Do you see what the little girl and boy are doing? (Pause.) That little girl is *mad*! What is she so mad about? (Wait and give students time to look and think.)

Information Literacy

Student: The little boy has the same picture. It looks like he copied.

LMT: Absolutely. There are times when you would be like the little girl. Wouldn't *you* be mad if you just solved the toughest problem in math class, but the person behind you copied your answer, turned it in, and got credit for what should have been *your* best effort? (Heads nod.)

There are other times when you would be like the little boy. When? (Rhetorical, momentary pause.) Let's say you have a paper due tomorrow and you haven't started it yet. You come check a book out of the library, go home, and happily copy away until you have something ready to turn in. Like the smug little boy, you are quite pleased with yourself. A few of you may not see anything wrong with that. I am not here to condemn you, at least not until I know that you have been taught how to fix this problem.

Now look at the teacher in the cartoon. (LMT reads the caption.) Who knows what is a copyright?

Student: Copyright is something that let's you copy?

LMT: I'm actually glad you said that. I heard someone say one time, "It's not when you copy wrong, it's when you copy... *right!*" It's actually quite the opposite, however. Other ideas?

Student: It's like a legal thing. Someone owns the book?

LMT: Now you're on track. Think about how hard it is for you to write a term paper. Now think about an author or artist who writes and creates all the time. Copyright is their legal protection for the work they have done. Look around you. Every single item in this room has a copyright. (LMT holds up a book.) Here on the back of the title page of this book is a little circle "c" with a date.

After all their hard work of writing, then finally getting something published, this author, and all the others in this room, are granted legal protection. They own their work and need to get paid for it because that is probably how they feed their families and earn a living. Your mom and dad bring home a paycheck, and you hit them up for a new pair of jeans. Well, how do you think authors provide for their families?

LMT: But what does this mean for you directly? What does copyright mean for *you* as you begin a research project?

Student: We shouldn't copy. (Students are usually listening quite intently at this point, if an anecdote relates copyright to their everyday situation.)

Lifelong
Skills

LMT: Yes. I think you see my point that it is actually illegal for you to simply take information out of a book. An advertisement I just heard on the radio yesterday compared it to picking up a book or CD in a store, zipping it into your backpack, and trying to walk out of the store without anyone knowing. You are literally stealing from the author. When you have a big project to do for school, our job today is to see how you can avoid being like that little boy in the cartoon. There is a simple thing he could have done so that the little girl would not have been quite so mad at him. (Pause.)

If the little boy in the cartoon had turned around and said, "I owe the whole idea for this wonderful work to my friend, Susie." I bet she wouldn't have been quite so upset. What I am saying is the point of this lesson: *Give credit!* How do you do that? (Rhetorical pause.)

You give credit to a source with something called a bibliography. We will have an activity today where I will not only show you what a bibliography is, but we will walk through the steps of exactly how to put one together, so when you come to this library media center in just a couple of days and begin to use these sources, you will be legal and not have any authors mad at you. You will know how to give them credit.

Formats and Sources

Timing: 5 minutes.

LMT: Before I get into bibliography, let's quickly cover the strategies for "Sources" on the Research Process sheet. My goal is for you to be able to follow this sheet yourself on future projects and have it make sense. You should be saying to yourself, "It's obvious that once I have a topic, I need places to look for information!"

Remember what you should be saying at every research process step: "But this is obvious!"

When you came to the LMC for orientation at the beginning of school I asked you, "What are the two kinds of things in this room, two general kinds of places where information comes from?" Besides fiction and nonfiction, we decided there were books and computers. Remember we said these had another name? (Pause, but for the sake of time, the LMT can't always wait for a student response. Wait just long enough for them to form an answer in their heads.) "Print," and... everything else. If it's not in print, it's usually electronic, which we call "nonprint." On your Research Process sheet, under "Sources," look at letter A. Does anyone know what a "format" is? (Pause.)

All information comes from sources, but a format is the particular kind of source in which information comes. Let me compare all the sources of information in this room to all the boxes of cereal on the grocery store shelves. These are all sources in the LMC, and it is all cereal on the shelves, but there are different *brands* of cereal, just as there are different *formats* of information sources. For example, let's take a look at the bibliography sheet. Books are a format of information. Reference books and encyclopedias are other formats, as are magazines and newspapers. For nonprint sources, CD-ROMs and the Internet are two different formats of electronic information.

Unlike when I was in high school, you live in a time when information comes in a wide variety of formats. We are here to make sure you explore all of them. That is why, when your teacher says, "You must have five sources for your bibliography," it is a bit misleading. What you need to know is that you absolutely cannot use only five books and then tell me you have everything you need for your report. That is like eating five bowls of Corn Pops everyday for breakfast for the rest of your life. You're going to get mighty tired of them. Think of all the other kinds of cereal you are missing! You may have five books, but think of all the facts about your topic that you're missing in other formats such as CD-ROMs or the Internet.

When your teacher and I planned the unit, we decided, based on the amount of time you have for this project, that it is reasonable to ask you for a minimum of five sources, but they must be in at least *three* formats. Does that make sense?

Student: But I have a computer at home and I've already found found five great web sites for my topic. Can't I use them?

LMT: Great question! Yes, you absolutely can, but that is only one format. You may use as many of any one format as you like, as long as you use at least one each of two other formats. You can have five boxes of Corn Pops as long as you also have a box of Rice Krispies and a box of Wheaties.

Being Prepared and Using Time Wisely

LMT: While you are at this school, you will always be required to use a combination of print sources as well as electronic sources. We want you to be prepared for anything any teacher may require of you, both in high school and beyond. Whether you plan on going to college or into the work force, at some point you will most likely be asked to access and use both print and nonprint information.

**Information
Literacy**

LMT: So (getting back to the student with the home computer), what you need to do now is locate your topic in some books. I always tell students to start with the easy formats first, such as encyclopedias, and then work your way toward the harder ones. Remember, research is *F-A-S-T*. Better not to be caught short. Another bit of advice for using your school time wisely is, if you have the Internet at home, don't use it here. Use your library time to locate those materials which exist for you only in this room. There may be some reference books, for example, which you will not be able to check out. Use those first when you start your research.

Research Requirements for Sources

Timing: 5 minutes.

LMT: Let's take just a moment to record project requirements on your Research Checklist (*Figure 6-2*). Look under "Sources" at letter A. As you can see, you need a minimum of three formats. Is everyone clear on that? Now look at letter B and record the number five on the blank line to show that you know you need at least five sources. Is everyone clear about the difference in the number of formats and sources that are required? As you begin your own research, please ask me to explain this again, anytime!

Your teacher will give you the due date for your sources and the number of points you'll receive for successfully completing this research step. Remember, we think you're smarter the more sources you use! This is usually a great way to get extra credit. Using more sources and formats than required shows your teacher that you are motivated, that you are interested in your topic, and that you know how to credit your sources properly. This leads us into an important activity.

Where Do Bibliographies Come From?

Timing: 5 minutes.

LMT: To keep the little girl in the cartoon happy, and to keep your teacher happy too, you need to know how to credit your sources. Take out the handouts called Bibliography: MLA Examples (*Figures 6-4, 6-5*). To try to be as accurate as possible, I've taken most entries on this sheet from an Internet MLA web site. Notice the web site is at the top of this page.

You need to know that other teachers may give you different versions of an MLA bibliography. That's okay! Sometimes MLA sources are slightly different. Isn't that strange? This guide sheet is subject to change at any time, as I'm always looking for versions which best match the MLA guides your teachers are using.

I've been saying, "MLA," but where do bibliographies come from? (Rhetorical pause.) MLA means that this one came from an organization called the Modern Language Association. In your school career, you may also receive a bibliography from APA, the American Psychology Association. What is important to remember is that bibliography styles only come from certain, official places:

What your teacher cannot do is make up a bibliography style in their head. They can't just say, "Oh, just put down the title, author, and page number. That's all I need for you to show you used something." Unless the bibliography style comes from an official source, such as MLA or APA, you have every right to tell the teacher, "There's a better way!"

LMT: Once you realize that every teacher in every class for every research project wants you to do a bibliography correctly, you'll keep these style pages with you for the rest of your life! Just think how impressed next year's teachers will be with you when you, say, "Oh, I know how to do that!" So let's do it.

Lifelong Skills

Fig. 6-4. Bibliography: MLA Examples

Except for starred items, all examples are from the following web site:

12 Feb. 1999 <http://ollie.dcccd.edu/library/Module4/M4-V/examples.htm>.

BOOKS:

No author*

People of Long Ago. Milwaukee: Rourke Publishers, 1986.

One author*

Newberry, Louis. Hair Design. Los Angeles: Newberry Press, 1986.

Two authors

Zwerdling, Alex, and Richard Voorhees. Orwell and the Left. New Haven: Yale UP, 1974.

More than two authors*

Kingsley, Eric, et al. Ships. New York: Alfred A. Knopf, 1995.

Edited

Foster, Carol E., Mark A. Siegel, and Nancy R. Jacobs, eds. Women's Changing Role. The Information Series on Current Topics. Wylie: Information Plus, 1990.

By a corporation*

Dallas County Community College District. Richland College. Institutional Self-Study. Dallas: Richland College, 1993.

SPECIAL BOOKS:

Anthology or multi-volume set

"Fromm, Erich 1900-1980." Contemporary Authors. Vol. 29. New Revision Series. Detroit: Gale, 1990. 55 vols. to date. 1981- .

Atlas

Atlas of the World. New York: Oxford UP, 1992. Munro, David, ed.

Dictionary

"Hard Rock." The American Heritage Dictionary of the English Language. 3rd ed. Boston: Houghton, 1993.

Poem, play, or short story from an anthology

Chekhov, Anton. The Cherry Orchard. Trans. Avraham Yarmolinsky. Norton Anthology of World Masterpieces. Ed. Maynard Mack. 4th ed. Vol. 2. New York: Norton, 1979. 1192-1230. 2 vols.

ENCYCLOPEDIAS:

In print, with author

Landry, Tom. "Football." World Book Encyclopedia. 1991 ed.

In print, no author

"Industrial Architecture." New Caxton Encyclopedia. London: Caxton, 1977. 20 vols.

Fig. 6-5. Bibliography: MLA Examples

CD-ROM:
Encyclopedia article
Kumbier, William A. "Science Fiction." <u>World Book 1997 Multimedia Encyclopedia</u>. Deluxe ed. CD-ROM. 1997 ed.

Newspaper article
Birnbaum, Mary C. "Information-Age Infants: Technology Pushes the Frontiers of What Babies Know." <u>Dallas Morning News</u> 23 Aug. 1994: 5C. <u>NewsBank CD News</u>. CD-ROM.

INTERNET:
Web site
"Hank Aaron." 1996. <u>Total Baseball</u>. Tot@lSports. 6 May 1997 <http://www.totalbaseball.com>.

Encyclopedia article
Enfield, David B. "El Niño." <u>Britannica Online</u>. Vers. 98.2. Apr. 1998. Encyclopedia Britannica. 1 Jul. 1998 <http://www.eb.com>.

Magazine article
Kluger, Jeffrey. "The Gentle Cosmic Rain." <u>Time</u>. 9 Jun. 1997. 11 Jun. 1997 <http://www.pathfinder.com/index.htm>.

Newspaper article
Johnson, George. "Don't Worry: A Brain Still Can't Be Cloned. " <u>New York Times</u>. 2 Mar. 1997, forums sec. 11 Jun. 1997 <http://forums.nytimes.com/library/national/0302clone-review.html>.

E-mail
Jeser-Skaggs, Sharlee (sjs@dcccd.edu). "Keyword Quirks." E-mail to Gary Duke (gd@dcccd.edu). 28 Feb. 1995.

MAGAZINES:
Article, with author
Idelson, Holly. "Gun Rights and Restrictions." <u>Congressional Quarterly Weekly Report</u>. 24 Apr. 1993: 1021-27.

Article, no author
"Stolen Art Treasures Found in Texas." <u>Facts on File</u>. 22 Jun. 1990: 459.

NEWSPAPERS:
Article, with author
Moreno, Sylvia. "Senate Endorses Gun Bill after Brief Filibuster." <u>Dallas Morning News</u>. 18 May 1993: 1A+.

Article, no author*
"Aiding the Arts." <u>The Milwaukee Sentinel</u>. 15 Jan. 1997: 3B

MISCELLANEOUS
Film and video
<u>The Wrong Stuff: American Architecture</u>. Videocassette. Dir. Tom Bettag. Carousel Films, 1983.

Interview
Face to face: Pei, I. M. Personal interview. 27 Jul. 1983.
Telephone: Poussaint, Alvin F. Telephone interview. 10 Dec. 1980.

Pamphlet
Treat like a book.

MLA Bibliography Examples for Print Materials

Literacy

Timing: 5 minutes.

LMT: Let's take a look on the overhead at the Bibliography: MLA Examples (*Figures 6-4, 6-5*). Our goal in this lesson is for you to be able to understand all the parts and pieces of a bibliography entry and be able to use this guide sheet as a clear reference in the future. First, be sure you are on the sheet that starts with "Books." Notice this sheet is divided by the formats we were talking about earlier. (LMT slides a marker down the sheet and reads the format section titles.) Get ready to put check marks beside the print materials I think you will use most often.

- **Books:** Put a check underneath "Book" beside "With one author." Like this example I have here (LMT holds up a typical World War II nonfiction book), many of you will find that the book you're using was written by only one person. Just in case the book you locate is different, look at the MLA sheet, and it shows you what to do if a book has two authors, more than two, or if it doesn't have an author at all but was put together by an editor or a corporate group. You need to be able to handle anything. This sheet will show you exactly what to do! Does that make sense?

- **Encyclopedias:** Put a check mark beside both an encyclopedia article "with author" and "no author." For the sample activity we are going to do today the author will be very apparent. Unfortunately, sometimes you won't be able to find one and the guide sheet will help you in either case.

- **Magazines:** On the next sheet locate the "Magazines" section. Be aware that these entries may be helpful for those of you who are able to locate primary sources, or authentic magazines, from World War II. For example, you are very lucky that this library media center has an archive of original *Life* magazines from the war years. On the MLA sheet, notice there are entries for magazine articles both with or without an author.

- **Newspapers:** We will not put a check mark here today, but some of you may be able to locate primary source newspaper articles in other libraries. Perhaps your grandparents have old newspapers stashed in the attic!

MLA Bibliography Examples for Nonprint Materials

LMT: Your MLA sheet also covers nonprint materials, usually electronic or computer sources (*Figure 6-5*). We want you to be prepared, for example, if your class just happens to show a video and it's about your topic! Take out a piece of paper and jot down notes. Then get the bibliography information after class and give credit for it! In another case, even if you just use one picture from a CD-ROM, you need to give credit for it. Besides staying within copyright regulations, as we just learned, your teacher will think you're smarter the more sources you use. It's a win-win situation, and this little piece of paper is your guide (again holding up the MLA sheet).

Information Literacy

- **CD-ROMs:** Locate the CD-ROM section on the guide sheet. Put a check mark beside the entry for an encyclopedia article on CD-ROM because that is the principal kind of general CD-ROM source we have available in this library media center. However, we also have a specialty CD-ROM just on World War II which may contain some primary source information.

Technology Proficiency

- **Internet:** The last item you see is the Internet. This is what everyone wants to use. Put a check mark here because we will make sure everyone has an opportunity, during your scheduled research time, to use the Internet so that we prepare you with this important information skill. Exactly how to credit this source will also be part of our hands-on bibliography activity.

Fig. 6-6. Bibliography Activity

Name_____ Teacher _____

Alphabetical order _____

Bibliography: Encyclopedia

Author *if available* (last name, first name, middle) _____ (period)

Article title ("quotation marks") _____ (period)

Title of encyclopedia (<u>underlined</u>) _____ (period)

Year_____ followed by: *ed* (period)

Example: Barnes, Isaac Jacob. "Camels." <u>The World Book Encyclopedia</u>. 1996 ed.

- -

Alphabetical order _____

Bibliography: CD-ROM Encyclopedia

Author *if available* (last name, first name) _____ (period)

Article Title ("quotation marks") _____(period)

CD-ROM Title (<u>underlined</u>) _____(period)

Edition (abbreviate the word edition) _____(period)

Write the words: *CD-ROM* (period)

Year_____ followed by: *ed* (period)

Example: Adams, Ernest D. "Spanish Armada." <u>The World Book Multimedia Encyclopedia</u>.
Deluxe ed. CD-ROM. 1998 ed.

- -

Alphabetical order _____

Bibliography: Internet Web Site

Title of web site ("quotation marks") _____ (period)

Date of access: Day (numeric) Month (abbreviated) Year _____ (no period)

URL (<web site address in brackets>) _____ (period)

Example: "Watergate." 5 Oct. 1998 <http://www.cnn.com>.

From *Practical Steps to the Research Process for High School* © 1999 Libraries Unlimited. 800-237-6124.

Student Activity: Bibliography

Reference

Timing: There is usually only about 5 or 10 minutes to demonstrate this first example for reference using an encyclopedia.

LMT: Let's not talk anymore about a bibliography; let's do one! On the overhead now I have what I sometimes call a "cheat sheet" (*Figure 6-6*). That's because I bet you haven't seen fill-in-the blanks for a while. This may be the only time for the rest of your life that anyone actually walks you through these incredibly tiny parts and pieces of a bibliography. It will be worth your while to hold your attention for the next few minutes.

Let me start with a few quick directions. Notice the stack of encyclopedias in the middle of your tables. Take a minute and put one volume between partners. You will be using that volume to locate the bibliography information we identify. But do not record information from your volume on your activity sheet; only record what I write on the overhead. The reason for this is that I will purposely find bibliography information that is even more complicated than what is indicated on the activity sheet. I want you to be prepared for anything you encounter in your own research. Does this make sense?

As you look at the activity sheet, notice that "Author" is the first item. The author is the most important part of a bibliography entry because that is from whom you would be stealing information if you did not give credit! Whenever an author's name is available, it will *always* be the first item in a bibliography, and it will be used later to put the entry in alphabetical order. Many students skip over an author when using an encyclopedia because they don't think there is one. That's why we're using this particular encyclopedia. It is excellent at giving full name credit to each one of the thousands of authors who wrote the individual articles throughout all the volumes.

Open your volume to any two-page spread where the two guide words at the top are *different*. If they're the same, it's a large article and you need to keep turning pages until the guides words are different. (Spot check students for following directions, but depend on the classroom teacher to circulate and give assistance.)

Slide your finger down the columns until you get to the end of an article. There you will see in teeny, tiny letters a person's name, and that is the author of that particular article. Is everyone finding those tiny little names? Your teacher will walk around and assist those of you in the back while I walk around the front area. (LMT takes a few minutes to spot-check that partners are pointing to an author.)

LMT: Now, everyone, close your books! (Wait a moment for this to happen.) Good. Get ready to copy onto the activity sheet what I will write here on the overhead. Let me see, I have the "N" volume and the entry I located is for a person you may have heard of, "Sir Isaac Newton." Here is an author, "John Q. Jones," at the bottom of the article. Both the activity sheet and the MLA sheet tell you to write the last name first, so please write on your sheet: Jones. The guide sheets show you there is a comma after the last name, so do that. Next write the author's first name, "John." Now this person also has a middle initial, "Q," followed by a period. So write that in the natural order in which it would follow after the first name. Someone raise your hand and tell me what would happen if the person's middle name was written out.

Student: Can't we just skip the middle name?

LMT: I'm very glad you asked that because I'll answer you with a story.

Pretend it is the first day of school and you are my class. As you come into the room I begin to write down your names on the board to make a seating chart. While I'm writing you say,

"Hey, that's not the way I spell my name!"

*"Too bad," I answer. "That's how it sounds to me so that's what I'll put! (The students are really staring at me.) Class, can I do that? (Rhetorical pause.) Can I just **decide** to spell **your** name wrong? Of course not! It's **your** name. If I spell it wrong, it's not even you anymore, it's someone else."*

Do you get my point? That is what happens when you simply decide to leave off part of, or misspell, an author's name. You don't have that right, any more than I would have had the right to simply decide to spell your name wrong. Makes sense?

Now the entire name group is punctuated by a period at the end, notice on the sheet? Let's move on to the next item which is, "Article title." Someone tell me what an article title is?

Student: The title of the article.

LMT: Yes, but what is that in particular?

Student: Your topic.

LMT: Exactly. It's what you're looking up, or it's a keyword to your subtopic question. I've purposely picked a harder one as my example. Remember I said I had the "N" volume with the entry, "Sir Isaac Newton?" The last name appears first whenever you look up a person in a general reference book, so copy onto your activity sheet, "Newton." Notice that a comma always follows the person's last name. The first name and middle name or initial must appear exactly as it does in the encyclopedia, but in this case, there is a title preceding the first name. You would need to record it in the natural order, exactly as it appears, "Sir Isaac," following the last name. Remember, don't become so involved with the order of names that you forget to spell correctly. Finally, notice the MLA sheet shows you there is again a period at the end of the article title. Everyone with me?

The next item on the sheet is "Title of encyclopedia." Whew! Finally something simple. Well, not so fast. Here on the spine it says an abbreviated name for the reference, but when we turn the book to the front cover, it states a full name. That is what you have to put! You must always look a book over and find the entire title, not to be confused with a series title. No shortcuts, or again you'd be simply deciding to change the name. I usually tell students to check inside on the title page which very clearly states what you're looking for.

I'm going to put aside the overhead for a minute. (LMT holds up an encyclopedia volume where everyone can see.) Let's locate the remaining item—the year—inside the volume. Everyone open up your volume to the title page. You can identify it because it has much more information on it than just the title. In fact, it has all of the bibliography pieces we need to find.

Under the title, what is different from regular books, is the absence of an author. We've already found that authors in encyclopedias usually follow directly after each article. What is the same as regular books, for you to be aware of, is that the publisher and place of publication are located at the very bottom of the title page. See them? What happens if four cities are listed, as they are here?

Student: You write all four?

LMT: Actually, there is a rule here that will make your life very easy. You pick the first one. That's it! You don't even have to think about the rest. (LMT looks around for a quick visual comprehension check.) You'd need to know that for a book's bibliography entry, but it doesn't call for that information here for an encyclopedia.

So let's get back to the year. Turn the title page over to the back. Somewhere buried in all the small print is always a date. Look, we have a problem again. There are tons of dates here in this encyclopedia. Which one do we pick this time?

Student: The first one?

LMT: Not this time. Anyone else?

Student: The last one?

LMT: Yes, if you mean the latest date. Remember, doesn't it make sense that you're looking for the date this particular book was printed? The latest date refers to, of course, the newest information.

Student: Shouldn't I just look for the little circle "c" for copyright?

LMT: Yes, a book is usually copyrighted each time it is published, but the true criteria is the latest date you see.

LMT: Let's record everything we've found onto the activity sheet. As I am writing each item, try to correct me if I miss the specific punctuation for each one. (Students watch closely to see if I goof up, which I do, on purpose!) This is extremely important for an accurate bibliography entry. Let me tell you a story that may help this make sense.

Today's Tuesday. Can you walk into your math teacher's class and say, "Hello teacher. It's Tuesday, and I've decided that for today, 2 + 2 = 5"?

Just like you're looking at me now, your teacher would probably look at you like you're crazy. The reason I tell you this is that it is just as crazy for you to say, "Teacher, it's Tuesday, and I've decided for this project, I am not going to put a colon after the place of publication."

You simply cannot do that! Who says so? (Pause.) MLA says so. This does not make your life harder. We are never expecting you to memorize all this. That is what this MLA guide sheet is for. Just copy it! Are you beginning to realize how this little piece of paper will save your life? This may sound like it's off the deep end now, but the more you do bibliography entries correctly, the less weird it will seem. It's no more weird than copying all the little bits and pieces of a web site URL correctly.

Finally, the sheet calls for you to add the letters "ed" with a period after the year. When you read this back, it says, "The 1998 edition." We're done! You'll know how to do this for the rest of your life!... at least for an encyclopedia. You've been great listeners. Did everyone get all of this reference bibliography information copied onto your activity sheet? Remember this is an example page for you to keep in your binders. I have individual bibliography cards in bins around the library media center at key locations near the type of source they match with. Help yourself anytime, for any class.

We've run out of time for today. The bell is about to ring. We will quickly cover the remaining two bibliography examples at the beginning of tomorrow's lesson. Please stack up your encyclopedias.

CD-ROM

These last two examples are usually completed the next day at the beginning of Lesson 3, using Figure 6-6.

LMT: Let's move down the activity sheet to the CD-ROM example which we can cover more quickly. Once again, copy my information as I write on the overhead, because I will give you a more complicated example than the activity sheet indicates.

For this project, I want you to be aware of at least three kinds of CD-ROMs available for you to use. First, I definitely want each one of you to look up your topic in a general reference CD-ROM, the example we'll do together. I know these references are often available online, but remember, we are here to expose you to a variety of formats of sources, so use the CD-ROM.

Second, you could check for your topic in the topic specific CD-ROM, exclusively on World War II, which is already set up for your class at the stand-alone CD-ROM computer station. (LMT points out this station.) Third, there are magazine articles available on CD-ROM periodical databases. Like many other libraries, we do not have the storage space for back issues of magazines, so you need to learn to locate magazine articles electronically. A sample bibliography entry for a magazine article on CD-ROM is on your MLA guide sheet.

Let's quickly fill in the CD-ROM data on your activity sheet. By the way, where does the bibliography information for a CD-ROM come from? (LMT looks inquiringly around the class.) From a printout! Since we have a small charge for per page printouts here, you need to bring a little bit of change with you on research days. I happen to have an overhead transparency of a sample CD-ROM general encyclopedia printout and one for a periodical (magazine) CD-ROM database. Many of the bibliography parts, and even the punctuation, are similar to the print encyclopedia, but there are some important differences to be aware of.

LMT:
- The article title for an electronic encyclopedia is often the same keyword entry that you used with a printed encyclopedia. However, on an electronic magazine article title, be aware there is a big difference. Record the actual title of the article as it appeared in the magazine, not just your keyword entry.

- The CD-ROM title is pretty straightforward. See it here on the bottom of the printout? (LMT circles the CD-ROM title on the overhead transparency.) Just copy it. If printout information is ever confusing, please ask me to help you. Underline the title as you do with the main title of any source, then put a period.

- Next is the edition. See if it is located on your printout. If not, you are not held accountable for information which does not directly appear. Abbreviate edition to "ed" with a period.

- Next, simply write, "CD-ROM," also with a period.

- The year is when this general encyclopedia CD-ROM was published, again followed by the abbreviation "ed." It would read, "The 1998 edition." If you get confused, take a look at the example written directly underneath each bibliography fill-in-the-blank activity area, as well as to your MLA guide sheet.

Internet

Timing: As quickly as possible.

LMT: The last sample entry we will do together is for an Internet web site. Everyone will use the Internet as one of your three basic formats of information for this project so that you gain experience in searching and evaluating web sites. As with most electronic information, you will need a printout from the Internet to locate bibliography information. I have an overhead transparency here from a Holocaust web site, which I bookmarked on the computers, to show you as an example. Since we are going to focus on a web site today, you'll need to consult the MLA guide sheet for other types of Internet citations.

Compared to the bibliography entries we have just completed, this one is very simple. There are only three items which absolutely must be included in an Internet web site bibliography entry: the title of the web site, the date of access, and the URL, which is the web site address. Here are a few helpful hints.

First, locate and correctly copy all parts of the web site title, remembering the punctuation as it appears on your activity sheet. Second, locate the date of access, usually printed in the upper or lower right-hand corner of the printout. If it's not there, remember, it's simply today's date, meaning the date you actually locate and print the information. Record the day first with no punctuation, then the month abbreviated to three letters with a period (LMT is writing this on the overhead), then the year with no period.

Third, locate the URL—the web site address—in the Locator bar directly above the web site window. The URL also appears at the top of the printout and always starts with, "http://." It is extremely important to copy correctly. URLs are case and space sensitive. In other words, do not add spaces or capital letters where they do not appear. Finally, enclose the URL in angle brackets. (LMT draws parenthesis on the overhead.) Are these brackets?

Student: No!

LMT: Correct. (The LMT demonstrates square brackets, [ ], and angle brackets, < >.) Be careful not to confuse brackets with parenthesis.

Student: How can I remember all this?

LMT: Great question. It seems tedious and overwhelming. As we said earlier, you never need to memorize this. Bibliography activity cards, "cheat sheets," are in bins around the library media center if you feel you need them to correctly gather and create an accurate bibliography entry. However, remember our goal has been for you to read and understand the Bibliography: MLA Examples sheet. Those are also always available here in the LMC. Come ask for one any time, for any class. Just follow and copy each entry exactly as it appears. What is the key to selecting which entry form to use?

Student: The format of information you're using... and how many authors?

LMT: You guys are fantastic! I'll see you tomorrow to learn notetaking strategies.

Notes

1. "Modern Language Association (MLA) Guide to Style." 2 Jul. 1998 <http://www.wilpaterson.edu/wpcpages/library/mla.htm>.

2. "American Psychological Association, APA PsycNET." 12 Jul. 1998 <http://www.apa.org/about/>.

Chapter 7

Reading, Thinking, and Selecting: Lesson 3, Part 1

Instructor

Student Lesson

"Hmmm... what does this note say?"
—Student deciphering
his own note

Fig. 7-1. Research Process: Read/Think/Select

Topic
- A. Locate topic ideas in grade-level texts, unit concepts, current literature studies.
- B. Check in the library media center for sources to determine supporting information.
- C. Cross-check in an encyclopedia to narrow or broaden a topic.
- D. Create a thesis statement to investigate the topic.

Subtopics
- A. Ask yourself: What do I want to know about my topic?
- B. Specific: Pre-search encyclopedia or nonfiction book's table of contents for ideas.
- C. General:
  - Thing: who, what, when, where, why/how.
  - Person: early life, education, accomplishments, later life.
- D. Minimum of three subtopics; maximum is determined by time and information.
- E. List subtopics in outline form by Roman numeral. Construct outline guide.

Sources
- A. Source: Anything used for information.
  - Format of sources:
    - Print: books, references, magazines, newspapers, maps, charts, etc.
    - Nonprint: videos, software, CD-ROMs, Internet.
- B. Number of formats (minimum of three). Number of sources.
- C. Credit sources using an official guide such as the MLA Bibliography sheet.
- D. Know the difference:
  - Primary vs. secondary sources.
  - Regular vs. annotated bibliography.

Read/Think/Select
- A. Read an entire "chunk" *before* selecting facts. Put your pencil down!
- B. Think about what was read. What was important?
- C. Select appropriate information from each "chunk."

Notetake
- A. Note cards: One note per card! Title cards with subtopics.
- B. Notebook Paper: Bullet or mark each note. Do not number notes at this time.
- C. Record only important facts or keywords.
- D. Discard small words like *a*, *an*, and *the*. Use commas and dashes instead.
- E. No sentences!
- F. Use quotation marks when copying. Give credit with source and page number.
- G. Alternative information gathering includes paraphrasing or summarizing.

Sort and Number Notes
- A. Sort notes by subtopic, by paragraph ideas, and then by supporting details (outline).
- B. Read all your notes. Select good notes; discard irrelevant notes.
- C. Sequence notes for fluent writing.
- D. Number all notes consecutively from section to section.

Extension
Write/Publish/Present
Final bibliography
Technology integration

Evaluation

From *Practical Steps to the Research Process for High School* © 1999 Libraries Unlimited. 800-237-6124.

Chapter Concepts

Promoting Literacy and Information Literacy

Educational reform can meet the literacy challenge of a diverse student population through the Research Process which is structured so that students must read, evaluate, and critically select information in order to proceed to the next step of notetaking. The reading, thinking, and selecting strategies in this chapter guarantee that the current dilemma of students either copying from print sources or printing electronic information and passing it off as their original work cannot occur!

Students Must Read to Process Information

Refer back to *Figure 1-2* to see that opportunities for reading diverse materials occur at each step of the Research Process. Strategies for the reading of research information, as opposed to pleasure reading, are the focus of this chapter.

Students Must Think About the Reading to Process Information

This step involves current brain research. How is information accessed, interpreted, and reshaped to meet a student's specific purpose?

Students Must Select Important Ideas and Keywords to Process Information

This step prevents plagiarism! Plagiarism may occur when students do not have the strategies to critically evaluate information in order not only to select what *is* important, but to know what to *leave out*! Without predetermined essential questions keyworded into subtopics, students do not have a frame of reference for information management. Without reading and thinking strategies, students do not process information to sort it, select it, and change its form to make it their own. It is when information changes form that learning occurs.

Instructor Information

Reading

Literacy

The value of the Research Process to promote literacy across all grade levels, ability levels, interest levels, and language needs cannot be overstated. If the teachers at your school site had any idea how much breaking research down into these manageable steps, then teaching the students strategies for accomplishing those steps, ties in to the overall educational literacy goals, they would be beating down the library media teacher's door.

As an example, I will relate an incident which occurred in my fifth year of collaborative research instruction. Though not a high school class, the value of the literacy experience is the same. The class was seated in the library media center, the teacher was rotating among the students to assist with direction following. That day the site reading specialist, who was also the Title I teacher, had scheduled to come and observe a student mainstreamed from the pull-out reading program. She was seated inconspicuously to the rear of the class.

The students had been taught and walked through the reading strategies seen in the following student lesson. The LMT had talked about how to read quickly through a "chunk" of text with pencils down. The students were all using a reference encyclopedia on this particular day and were seated in pairs. The classroom teacher had partnered high-level readers with struggling readers, so whenever necessary, a student was reading aloud to the partner. After reading, students discussed what they had just read. They decided what information matched the subtopic and what was important enough to copy onto their note cards. They then picked up their pencils and recorded their own notes.

Everyone was on task. Everyone completed the information gathering goal for the period despite the variety of reading ability levels for that kind of source. A check of students' notes reflected that information had been read, comprehended, selected, and recorded.

At the end of the lesson, the reading specialist came to me and said, "That was amazing! Do all the teachers at the school know about this? Do you know how much this ties in so completely with the reading strategies we teach them in special training? Those kids were reading because not only did it have purpose, but they were interested! How many times do you see students who are having fun reading an encyclopedia?" She went on to say that if more students were involved in an active library media program, there would not be as many reading difficulties. What a great asset to educational reform!

My response was that this is the curriculum of all library media teachers! That is why this position is so important, not only for research and technology integration into the curriculum but, as she saw first-hand, to support the school's literacy program. In providing experiences for reading for purpose as well as for pleasure, or reading in a variety of print and electronic formats, library media teachers offer an unbeatable integrated curriculum of both literacy and information literacy!

Reading strategies for research can include:

Information Literacy

- **Purpose:** Subtopics provide specific reasons for reading.

- **Speed:** Skim or scan instead of reading slowly.

- **Amount:** Read a "chunk" without stopping. Depending on reading ability, this means a paragraph, a page, or several pages.

- **Pencils down:** Reading without writing automatically promotes an uninterrupted sequence of reading, evaluating, and selecting important information.

Of special significance is the adaptation of these research reading strategies to the needs of special students. Reading specialists, Title I teachers, and ELL (English Language Learner) teachers are all able to include collaboration with the library media teacher on a research project as documentation in student IEPs (Individual Educational Programs). The regular classroom teacher is able to use examples of research process projects for site review or accreditation documentation for the integration of literacy (reading, writing, listening, speaking) and information literacy into the content-area curriculum.

ELL/Special Modifications

Content-Area Standard

Thinking

In my experience, the most common complaint among teachers in every subject area at my high school was, "Their work looks like they didn't even think about it!"

Not only do the students who come into the library media center not want to read for research, they don't voluntarily indulge in critical thinking. I do not think this is always their fault, or that they are simply lazy! I strongly believe they have not been equipped with the strategies which empower them to effectively read, evaluate, and select information. An essential question this entire book addresses is: Who should teach these skills? Because content-area teachers are already overwhelmed with their own curricular agendas, I advocate that teaching critical reading and thinking using the Research Process is the job of the library media teacher.

Problem Solving

Critical thinking strategies in the Research Process involve processing information by:

- Reading
- Comprehending
- Evaluating
- Selecting and prioritizing

Each one of these steps has definite strategies which are simple, even intuitive. But they *must* be taught!

Lifelong Skills

One of my collaborating teachers commented, "This is like riding a bicycle. It's easy to learn, and they'll never forget it. This [series of lessons] has changed their lives."

The on-task behavior, even the enthusiasm, that is displayed by students after this series of research lessons convinces me that all they needed was to be equipped with the proper tools for performing the task. I honestly had a sixth-grade class, at the conclusion of their entire project, ask the teacher, "When can we come back and do another one?" My high school students smirk at that story, but after a few days of working on their own, their attitude toward research visibly improves. You *can* teach kids to think!

Selecting

I have heard it said that teachers are really frustrated actors. This lesson on selecting important information from context is one where I pull out all the stops on dramatic instruction to emphasize to the students certain points about information evaluation strategies.

Purposeful evaluation strategies can include:

- Choosing information that directly supports the topic and subtopics

- Focusing on new information, not on obvious or prior knowledge, or small words your brain already knows

- Using a book's table of contents or index to go directly to subtopic information

- Using the bold sub-headings of encyclopedias to go directly to subtopic information

- Skipping information not related to subtopics, at least until subtopics have been covered

Specific strategies for selecting, excluding, or changing information are covered more explicitly in the chapter on notetaking.

Unlike lower grades where I alternate research instruction with a supporting activity, with high school students I must settle for demonstrating in the student lesson a reading, thinking, or selecting strategy which they will perform independently. With only one chance to make a lasting impression, the dramatic technique of instructional hyperbole becomes very important. An example is when I demonstrate how to skim and scan. I come around from behind the overhead and stand right in front of the class. While holding a book open to a page of text, with exaggerated facial expressions, voice intonations, and gestures, I actually say things like,

"I'm skimming quickly down the page... read, read, read, read. When I get to the bottom, I ask myself, "What was on this page? Absolutely nothing! So I flip to the next page and do it again."

I do not feel I am insulting students' intelligence by using words and gestures as if I were acting out the activity in a play. I think this play-acting enables me to make the same points lesson after lesson with the same sincerity and vigor. My exaggerations rivet their attention, and the students focus on what is being said whether they intend to or not. The students' ability to repeat evaluation strategies when working on their own testifies that something is working!

Problem Solving

What's interesting is the effect of the lesson on the class's instructor. Though I may repeat the same research lesson five times in one day, the same collaborative teaching partner not only remains with the students, but often comes up to me after each lesson to reflect on a different point or impression that he or she realized helps students gain these lifelong skills.

Lifelong Skills

 **Student Lesson**

Getting Started

Timing: A few minutes of reteaching for continuity.

LMT: Welcome to day three. Let's make some sense about what we've done for the last two days by looking back at the first few steps on your Research Process sheet (*Figure 7-1*). You may be surprised how much you have learned in a short time:

- Look at the first step, "Topic." For the rest of your life you'll have strategies for selecting a good topic for yourself. Challenge yourself and stretch your abilities, but choose a topic with information within your physical limitations, such as an after-school job or not having transportation to the public library, and with regard to your reading ability. Do not choose a topic so easy you learn nothing, or so difficult you get frustrated and cannot adequately complete the task.

- Look down at the next step, "Subtopics." You now realize that subtopics, which may be the keywords to essential questions your research will answer, are something you absolutely can't proceed without. They are the backbone of your research without which you have no idea what you are doing! They will tell you what information to include and what information to skip. Remember that controlling your subtopics is how you control information. At any time during your research you can combine, change, add to, or eliminate them, but you must have them!

- Look next at the "Sources" step of the Research Process. You know how important it is to give credit to an author, and how much to your advantage it is as well! Best of all, you know how to construct an accurate MLA bibliography.

Can things get much better? Yes, they can! Today you are going to learn what to do with information from the sources you so carefully selected. I am going to use student work to teach you effective strategies for reading, thinking about, and evaluating information and then selecting facts for notetaking.

Fig. 7-2. Purposeful Reading Cartoon

"It's an 'audio alternative' called reading."

Reprinted with permission of H. L. Schwadron as appearing in *Phi Delta Kappan*.
January 1997, Volume 78, number 5.

Reading

Timing: 5 minutes.

Literacy

LMT: (With *Figure 7-2* on the overhead, LMT holds up a fat book about Winston Churchill.) Once you find a good source, guess what you've gotta do? You actually have to read even though, like the boy in the cartoon, there are many other things you'd rather do! Do you think that I am asking you to read this entire 350-page book? (Rhetorical pause.) No! That's the good news. This whole book may be about your topic, but what about those wonderful subtopics that tell you what to include and what to leave out?

ELL/Special Modifications

Do you again see how subtopics will save your life? Instead of having to read this whole book, you simply turn to the table of contents (LMT opens to this) or to the index (LMT locates this in the book), and you will see very quickly exactly what you need.

Oh, here is a chapter on my subtopic about Churchill's early war decisions. That's great. I know just what to do during this library period!

Student: What if that chapter is still more than I need?

LMT: Excellent question. Let's say the chapter is 30 pages long, and you only have 20 minutes left in the period. Do you have to sit here and read all 30 pages? Not really. There are a few, I'll call them "reading management" strategies that will save you from either unnecessary work or from being overwhelmed by too much information which might tempt you to give up critical evaluation and to plagiarize.

The first thing to think about is the word "read." Is that what you're really doing during research? No, this is not the same as relaxing at night with your favorite scary novel. What we should call this instead of "reading" is "skimming," which is reading quickly for the general idea, or even "scanning," which is glancing over text for quick concepts or answers to questions. So the first strategy is speed.

Lifelong Skills

LMT: The next strategy has to do with how much to read. Look on your Research Process sheet at letter A. The sheet says to read an entire "chunk" before selecting facts. What is a "chunk?" (Rhetorical pause.) Put your eyes back up on this book again and I'll show you something.

Problem Solving

Literacy

LMT: For students in high school, a "chunk" is at least a whole page. If you are a second language learner, a "chunk" may only be a paragraph. (LMT holds open a page of solid text.) For a second grader, a "chunk" might only be a sentence. That's only as much as he or she can read and think about at one time. For a fifth grader, it's probably a paragraph. But for you in tenth grade, it's at least a page and sometimes more than that. It is a judgment call that you'll get better at with practice. The size of a "chunk" for you depends on the amount of time you have, the difficulty of the book, the subtopic, and your ability to read and understand.

Remember how we eat our elephant one bite at a time? Dividing text into "chunks" gives you control when you are confronted with difficult or large amounts of information to read and comprehend.

You can't stuff a whole slice of pizza in your mouth at once, or you'd choke. That's exactly the same with information.

Thinking

Timing: 5 minutes or less.

LMT: The next strategy will help you think about what you have read. In other words, did you understand it? See this pencil in my hand? It's time to put it down! (LMT holds up a pencil, then dramatically sets it down on the closest table. Some students often follow suit, but it both gets their attention and helps get the point across.)

Did you know that if you physically have a pen or pencil in your hand when you get ready to read, you will automatically do what a pencil was intended to do: write! Instead, when you read a "chunk," the strategy of putting that pencil down, will automatically, magically, allow you to read that whole page.

In the beginning this is very hard to do. You'll have to force yourself. (Gestures are very effective here.) Hold your hand behind your back! What is the advantage of that pencil being down?

Student: You read!

LMT: That's it, but the good news is, you do even more than read. You actually start to think about what that "chunk" is saying.

Important Idea

With your pencil down, by the end of the "chunk," you're automatically saying to yourself, "I saw two facts that were important to my subtopic."

In other words, you are evaluating. You are doing by yourself what teachers are trying to teach you to do all through school: critical thinking. You're analyzing what's important, applying it to your topic and subtopics, and leaving out the rest.

Problem Solving

Selecting

Timing: 5 minutes or less.

LMT: When you evaluate information, what you are automatically doing is selecting what's important. Let me demonstrate how easy this is.

Here's a page about Winston Churchill. I skim quickly down the page, with my pencil down... read, read, read, read. When I get to the bottom, I think about my subtopic and automatically say, "Hmmm. There's nothing really important here!" So guess what I do? Turn the page!

Do you realize what has just happened? Without consciously trying, I read quickly, thought about what was on that page, and selected what was important, which in this case was nothing!

I do the same thing on the next page, but automatically, all by themselves, two important facts jump right off the page! They almost pick themselves!

Let me emphasize again, if you are writing while you are reading, you lose all that ability to make judgments about the information. Everything looks good. You stop reading quickly for general ideas, you stop evaluating for what is important, and pretty soon the bell rings, and you've spent the whole period copying a few pages of the book. While you sat there using 50 minutes to copy a few pages in one book, your neighbor who remembered to put her pencil down, used three sources! It's not brain surgery to know which student is going to end up with a more thorough project accomplished in less time.

Information Literacy

Do you see that by asking you to read your sources, we are not asking something unreasonable? The reading strategies just covered will help you any time you are confronted with the task of gathering and choosing information. These are tools to help you meet your teacher's goal for you to use your time wisely. Better than that, it meets your goal of learning to do research *F-A-S-T*. You want to finish this project, right?!

Chapter 8

Notetaking:
Lesson 3, Part 2

Student Lesson
Student Activities

"Notetaking prevents plagiarism!
Notetaking is learning."
— Deborah Stanley

Fig. 8-1. Research Process: Notetaking

Topic
    A. Locate topic ideas in grade-level texts, unit concepts, current literature studies.
    B. Check in the library media center for sources to determine supporting information.
    C. Cross-check in an encyclopedia to narrow or broaden a topic.
    D. Create a thesis statement to investigate the topic.

Subtopics
    A. Ask yourself: What do I want to know about my topic?
    B. Specific: Pre-search encyclopedia or nonfiction book's table of contents for ideas.
    C. General:
          Thing: who, what, when, where, why/how.
          Person: early life, education, accomplishments, later life.
    D. Minimum of three subtopics; maximum is determined by time and information.
    E. List subtopics in outline form by Roman numeral. Construct outline guide.

Sources
    A. Source: Anything used for information.
          Format of sources:
               Print: books, references, magazines, newspapers, maps, charts, etc.
               Nonprint: videos, software, CD-ROMs, Internet.
    B. Number of formats (minimum of three). Number of sources.
    C. Credit sources using an official guide such as the MLA Bibliography sheet.
    D. Know the difference:
          Primary vs. secondary sources.
          Regular vs. annotated bibliography.

Read/Think/Select
    A. Read an entire "chunk" *before* selecting facts. Put your pencil down!
    B. Think about what was read. What was important?
    C. Select appropriate information from each "chunk."

Notetake
    A. Note cards: One note per card! Title cards with subtopics.
    B. Notebook Paper: Bullet or mark each note. Do not number notes at this time.
    C. Record only important facts or keywords.
    D. Discard small words like *a, an,* and *the.* Use commas and dashes instead.
    E. No sentences!
    F. Use quotation marks when copying. Give credit with source and page number.
    G. Alternative information gathering includes paraphrasing or summarizing.

Sort and Number Notes
    A. Sort notes by subtopic, by paragraph ideas, and then by supporting details (outline).
    B. Read all your notes. Select good notes; discard irrelevant notes.
    C. Sequence notes for fluent writing.
    D. Number all notes consecutively from section to section.

Extension
          Write/Publish/Present
          Final bibliography
          Technology integration

Evaluation

From *Practical Steps to the Research Process for High School* © 1999 Libraries Unlimited. 800-237-6124.

Chapter Concepts

The Key to Information Ownership

Learning occurs when information changes form. Notetaking accomplishes this. Through the recording of keywords or facts, paraphrasing or summarizing, students must process the original information into a note which is then reprocessed into the writing of a rough draft. Information has changed form twice and plagiarism is impossible!

Recording a note necessitates that the student reads and comprehends information in order to evaluate and select it. These automatic and sequential steps *are* literacy and learning.

Literacy

Teaching Notetaking Strategies

High school teachers are overwhelmed with their own content-area curriculum. It is often social science and science teachers who assign the majority of research projects, but teaching research strategies is not in their curriculum. Therefore, the library media teacher should respond to the information literacy mandate to give direct instruction in information management strategies, including notetaking.

Notes Should Look Like Notes

Recording only keyword facts, on separate note cards or marked by dashes or bullets on notebook paper, is one way to eliminate plagiarism. Copying sentences is allowed only with quotation marks and endnote or footnote citations. Paraphrasing and summarizing are also legitimate forms of gathering information, but are not addressed in this book.

The Advantage of Good Notes

Speed, accuracy, and amount of information. Students can use more sources, take more notes, and later, sort notes more easily to write a better balanced and more internalized report.

Fig. 8-2. Notetaking Cartoon

"You're supposed to take notes... You can't send away for a transcript of today's class."

© 1998: Reprinted courtesy of Bunny Hoest and *Parade* magazine.

Student Lesson: Notebook Paper Notetaking

Timing: 20 minutes.

How Much Can I Copy in 45 Minutes?

LMT: Looking at your Research Process sheet (*Figure 8-1*), we'll move down from the "Read/Think/Select" section to the focus of today's lesson, on notetaking. The teacher in the cartoon on the overhead (*Figure 8-2*) says it best. She is telling her two little cyber-cherubs that they're, "supposed to take notes..." Something occurs in your brain when you take notes that is the secret to information ownership that does not have to remain a secret, as we'll see in a minute.

As soon as all your teachers construct a web page, someday it may be possible for you to sit at your home computer and send away for a transcript of each day's lesson, but is grabbing information electronically a legitimate means of solving your research problems? Is that a way to learn? What will you do tomorrow as you face a tangle of information?

Student: Copy it out of the book.

LMT: Very honest and very interesting. Your answer could be taken in two ways. Literally, it means information from a source goes right onto your page. Maybe you'd change a few words so you could tell your teacher you "summarized," but I think you mean that you need to transfer information from one place to another, right? Copying does not necessarily reflect a lack of honestly as much as a lack of strategies for evaluating and recording information. So let's dig into the Research Process toolbox again and construct some notetaking strategies.

First, there are a few simple directions for this part of the lesson. Take out five sheets of blank notebook paper. Does anyone have any idea why I said five sheets? (Pause.) Remember I told you on the first day that for this project you will need five subtopics.

Important Idea

Technology Proficiency

Information Literacy

Fig. 8-3. Sample Research Project Syllabus

Science Project Report

You have all semester to complete a science project. However, the research portion for the "Background Information" segment of the project is due in the next two weeks.

The topic of the paper will be the same as the focus of your science project. You are expected to use at least five sources of information, have at least three quotations supporting your research findings, and give credit in at least three footnotes.

Here is a list of the criteria and points for this research paper:

Title page	10 points
5-page typed paper	50 points
Quotes with footnotes	15 points
Visual image or chart	15 points
Bibliography	10 points

These criteria are very clear, however, see me during my conference hour (period 3) if you have any questions.

From *Practical Steps to the Research Process for High School* © 1999 Libraries Unlimited. 800-237-6124.

The Key to Learning: Information Ownership

LMT: Homework for the last two days was to choose between generic subtopics on the guide sheet, or to locate specific ones here in the LMC. Subtopics are essential for today's lesson, but are always changeable throughout your research. The key is this: Subtopics provide purpose. Once you know what you're looking for, the next problem is how to get the information (without copying).

The key issue for both researching and learning is to take information from a source and make it yours and not the author's. This is the whole point of today's lesson. It's almost the whole point of the entire Research Process. Does that make sense? Any time someone changes the form in which information comes, learning occurs. That is why copying is not learning. You will see there are strategies that are actually easier (and better) than copying!

Lifelong Skills

The answer to both essential issues—transferring information and making it your own—is notetaking. How many of you, somewhere in your school life, have had a teacher show you how to take notes? Because teachers have so much to teach you in their subject areas, they often think the "other" teacher should have covered this with you. Through no fault of their own, by this grade level they assume you know how to do notetaking. Therefore, most teachers give you a list of criteria for a project (*Figure 8-3*), telling you to locate good sources and write a great paper, right? Do you see now that there is a huge—we're talking Grand Canyon—hole between what you are to do and how you are to do it?

Believe it or not, we will fill the Grand Canyon today with easy notetaking strategies, a key part of information management. I have lots of student examples in this lesson that will help you understand what I'm talking about. So let's begin.

Information Literacy

Fig. 8-4. Copied Notes

Dewey Melvil (1851 -1931)
American librarian, who devised the Dewey De
mal System for classifying books in libraries..
He was born Melville Louis kossuth Dewey in
Adams center, N.Y.; on Dec 10, 1851. After gradı
from Amherst college in 1874, he served as a
librarian there for two years.
For the next seven years Dewey lived in Boston
where he was active in various organizations
for the improvement of library services and for
the promotion of spelling reform and of the use
of the metric system of measurement. From
1883 to 1888 he was librarian at Columbia Colle;
when Dewey moved to Albany in 1888 to become
director of the New York state Library, the sch
was continued in Albany as the New Y . State
Library school (It returned to Columbia University
in 1926)
In 1895, Dewey organized the Lake placid club in t
Adirondacks as a membership resort, and he founded
a similar club in Florida in 1927. He died at Lake
Placid, Fla, on Dec 26, 1931.
Dewey was a founder of the American Library Associ
(1876) and served at various times as its secr tary

From *Practical Steps to the Research Process for High School* © 1999 Libraries Unlimited. 800-237-6124.

Copied Notes

LMT: Look at your Research Process sheet (*Figure 8-1*) at the section about notetaking. The first thing to consider is: What do notes look like? (Momentary pause and eye contact with students.) The guide sheet says, "Bullet or mark each note." What this means is:

NOTES NEED TO LOOK LIKE NOTES!

I have a sample of student notes up here on the overhead (*Figure 8-4*). These are real notes taken by one of my library science students at the beginning of this year. (Long pause, to let the appearance of this example sink in.) Isn't this amazing? (LMT acts purposely astonished to contrast herself with the puzzled looks on many students' faces.) Some of you don't look so sure. I had one student in a previous class raise his hand and say quite honestly, "But that's the way my notes have *always* looked!"

Do these notes look like notes? (Brief pause to make eye contact with students.) Of course not! They look like what this person probably did: copy out of the book. (LMT slides her finger down the overhead while pointing out the following points on the page.) I didn't get mad at this student because he honestly didn't know any better, and besides, I knew I wanted to use his page as an example to show you, so I began to ask him questions.

I asked, "Besides the fact these don't look like notes, later on when you've taken notes from several other kinds of sources, how can you easily pick out what's important?" He just shook his head. He couldn't!

I said to him, (LMT points to a spot on the overhead.) "This looks like it's a date, which could have matched the subtopic of early life of this person. This, down here, looks like it could have been an accomplishment in Dewey's life." Then I asked, "How can you easily extract these facts and put them back together the way you'd like to talk about it in a report?" Again, he shook his head. He couldn't! Do you see that he'd almost have to take notes twice because everything is all jammed and jumbled up? This student is not in control of his information. It's controlling him!

Fig. 8-5. Notes Marked with Dashes

——— Dewey achieved order for a number of libraries in the world.

——— Dewey arranged his books based upon invention of Baconian order of history.

——— previous decimal arrangements did not impress Dewey because they were all based upon numbering shelves.

——— Dewey proposed to the Amherst Library Committee a new revolutionary way of arranging books.

——— The first university to adopt the new system was Columbia University.

——— Almost every library, including the library of congress used this system.

——— "Use of the classification system has spread outside the United States to all over the world."

From *Practical Steps to the Research Process for High School* © 1999 Libraries Unlimited. 800-237-6124.

Notes That Look Like Notes

For this demonstration, LMT uses overhead pens on transparency of Figure 8-5.

LMT: Here's another student's notetaking example (*Figure 8-5*). This is a little better. These are starting to look more like notes. See these marks on the side? (LMT goes down the page, using an overhead pen to emphasize the marks beside each note.) Each one of these is a note! That's easy to see. Students who copy out of the book often say, "My teacher will never know the difference!" But how hard is it to tell the difference between this (LMT flips overhead back to *Figure 8-4*) and this? (Again showing *Figure 8-5*.)

However, just because these look more like notes doesn't necessarily make them good. What is a "good" note? Look back on the guide sheet at letter C. It says, "Record only important facts or keywords." If we skip to letter E it says, "No sentences." Let's look back at the overhead example and see how it measures up. The first note says, "Dewey achieved order for a number of libraries in the world." What's wrong with that?

Student: It's a sentence, and he keeps repeating the topic, "Dewey."

LMT: Yes. The student was on the right track, but unless he is going to do letter F: "Use quotation marks when copying," or letter G: "Alternative information gathering includes paraphrasing or summarizing," these are unsatisfactory notes! Both C and G notetaking strategies require you to, as the sheet says, "Credit sources using an official guide," but your teacher has already told you that for this project footnotes or endnotes are not necessary. If you can't have any footnotes, guess what you can't do? (Pause for this to register.) You *cannot copy* even one sentence from any source for the entire research paper!

In the short time I have, I cannot demonstrate paraphrasing or summarizing with you. Does this mean you are absolutely not allowed to use these strategies for this project? You may, but your teacher will be checking off your notes when they're due, so he has final approval. These advanced notetaking skills may be a form of extra credit over and above the basic project requirements.

Fig. 8-6. Notes: Don't Be Too Brief

○	*Early life*
#3	• *born, Austrian town -- Braanau* • *father -- Aldis Hitler -- former name* • *mother -- Klara Polel -- peasant girl* • *father suffered tuberculosis, lived to 86*
○	
○	

From *Practical Steps to the Research Process for High School* © 1999 Libraries Unlimited. 800-237-6124.

Making a Bad Note Good

LMT continues to use overhead pens to make changes on Figure 8-4.

LMT: So we're back to square one. You must take real notes. We can figure out the strategies ourselves by picking apart this student's example. Let's change his bad note into a good note.

We already saw that this is a sentence. The obvious signals are the capital letter at the beginning and the period at the end. (LMT circles these on the overhead.) For those students who say, "My teacher will never know I copied," how long does it take to see a complete sentence in your notes? This is why I always encourage teachers to collect and flip through your notes before you begin to write. It is very obvious whether you've copied sentences, without even reading your notes!

Next you can cross out the word "Dewey." Why? Because this is the topic! Never, ever, ever repeat your topic in your notes. That is a waste of your valuable library time. You know your topic. Never repeat in notes what you already know. What are notes for? Gathering *new* information.

Let's read on: "achieved order for a number of... " Scratch out "for a" and instead put a dash. Look on your Research Process sheet at letter D: "Discard small words like *a*, *an*, and *the*. Use commas and dashes instead." We just saw how to do that. Only get used to leaving them out automatically when you are transferring sentence information from your source. For example, he says, "...libraries in the world." We know to scratch out "in the" and replace it with a dash.

Let's read this back. The new note says: "...achieved order—number of libraries—world." That is a keyword note. As the sheet says in letter C, "Record only important facts or keywords." However, be careful about eliminating too much when you record facts. Last week, a student was notetaking so conscientiously that her notes became too brief (*Figure 8-6*). Learn to combine keywords in different sentences and to select adjectives and descriptive phrases to create what I call, "fat, juicy notes!"

Fig. 8-7. Notes: Good Example

	RELIGION
◯ SOURCE #1	83%-HINDUS 11%-MUSLIMS NEXT LARGEST RELIGION -- CHRISTIANS, SIKHS, BUDDHIST TWO NATIONS -- INDIA+ JAINS PAKISTAN
SOURCE #2 ◯	HINDUS BELIEVE -- SOUL NEVER DIES HINDUS WORSHIP -- BRAHMA, CREATOR, UNIVERSE, VISHNU THE CATAGORIES -- BRAHMANS, SUDRAS
SOURCE #3 ◯	THE LOWEST JOB -- STREET SWEEPER LEATHER WORKER THE GOVERNMENT PROVIDED -- SCHOLARSHIPS JOBS ISLAM -- RELIGION OF THE MASSES SECOND LARGEST RELIGION INDIA -- SECULAR COUNTRY BIRTHPLACE OF HINDUS+ BUDDHISTS RELIGION -- IMPORTANT DATES;

From *Practical Steps to the Research Process for High School* © 1999 Libraries Unlimited. 800-237-6124.

The Purpose of Good Notes

LMT: These notes are looking great (*Figure 8-7*). The huge advantage of using "good" note strategies is speed. You will be able to record your notes much more quickly, covering more sources, more subtopics, and more information than the person who is sitting at the next table copying everything. As you saw in the first notetaking example (*Figure 8-4*), bad notes only hurt you by making the task of writing much more complicated.

Information Literacy

In the end, what is the real purpose of your notes? Are they for your teacher because you know he is going to collect and grade them? Absolutely not. The purpose of notes is to inspire you to write! The quality of a note directly relates to how much you can write from it. Does your teacher ever have to read your notes? Of course not! In 5 seconds per student he can flip through and do a simple check just for note construction. Then who are the notes for? You! Only you will ever read them. They only need to make sense to you, but they also need to contain all the information you will use to write your paper.

Literacy

Referring back to the short note example (*Figure 8-6*), let's see if these notes can make good sentences. Look at her first note: "Born, Austrian town—Braanau." I can make a sentence out of that: "[Her person] was born in the Austrian town of Braanau." But making one simple sentence isn't really enough. First, tap into your prior knowledge to add information. Second, retain those wonderful adjectives from your reading that create what I call "accurate interest." (LMT makes up a juicier sentence such as: [Her person] was born in poverty in the small mountain village of Braanau located in a remote section of Austria.)

The real key to good notes is the amount of information you know from them. Good notes are often called "keyword" notes. This is because the important facts you recorded should be the "key" to unlocking your brain so that tons of other things you already know, or read about, are added to the note. The result in high school is that you should be able to make many sentences from one good keyword note. In a way, a note is a mini-topic about which you tell everything you know. Here is an example: the word *adobe*. I'll bet I could sit down and write 10 pages right now just on what I know about adobe. In California history, I know what it is and what it was used for, where it came from, who made it, when it was used, and why it was used by the Spanish for their missions.

Lifelong Skills

Fig. 8-8. Research Checklist

LMT/Teacher Tracking	Points
Topic _____ (WW II) Holocaust _____	
Subtopics	

I. (What) was the Holocaust? _____

II. (Where) did it occur? _____

III. (When) did it happen? _____

IV. (Who) was involved? _____

V. (How) did it affect people & history? _____

Sources [ ]

   A. At least 3 formats (book, reference, interview, CD-ROM, Internet, etc.)
   B. Total number of sources: _____ 5 _____

Read and notetake [ ]
   A. At least 10 notes for each subtopic.
   B. Total number of notes: _____ 50 _____

Sort and number notes [ ]

Write rough draft from notes [ ]

LMT/Teacher Grading	
Title page	
Typed report	
Final bibliography	
Presentation activity	

From *Practical Steps to the Research Process for High School* © 1999 Libraries Unlimited. 800-237-6124.

Student Activity A: Preparing Notebook Paper Notes

LMT: I have an activity now for us to practice what we've been talking about. Tomorrow is your first day of real research. In this activity, we are going to prepare your actual notetaking pages. This is not fake. Your teacher and I planned that what we will do now will be the actual notetaking pages he will collect and check off on your Research Checklist sheet (*Figure 8-8*). I believe he has already told you a date when all your notes are due for a final check before we organize and outline them so you can begin writing.

You have five sheets of blank notebook paper. I have a couple of blank sheets here. (LMT puts a clear plastic sheet onto the overhead, draws a red margin line down the left side and a black line about an inch down from the top. This is repeated for a second blank page.) Why five sheets? Because you are required to have five subtopics. If your research time had been shorter, we would probably have only three subtopics and then only three sheets of paper. Get it? This is only to start with. Can you end up with more than five pages of notes? Of course.

Remember, this is *your* paper. You are in control now and know how to manage your own information. You may decide to give yourself six or seven subtopics, but prepare a notetaking sheet for each one. This is the way to do it. Put in front of you the Research Checklist (*Figure 8-8*). Before we go any further, let's fill in the blank space on the form for your notetaking goal. A simple guide is to aim for taking 10 notes per day. So in your five days of scheduled research, you should take a minimum of 50 notes, the number you can record on your sheet. That doesn't seem like much in high school. Don't forget this includes time spent locating and reading your sources. Fifty notes should enable you to easily write a five-page paper. You be the judge after that. The more notes you take, the more information you will have, and the easier it will be to write. This guideline gives you a way to budget your time. So what have we just given you? (Pause.) Another strategy for information management!

Information Literacy

Fig. 8-9. Final Bibliography

Bibliography

Dewey, Melvil. <u>Dewey Decimal Classification and Relative Index</u>. New York: Forest Press, Inc., 1958.

"Dewey, Melvil." <u>Microsoft Encarta '98 Encyclopedia</u>. CD-ROM. 1998 ed.

Ferguson, Anna Marie. "Historical Highlights from the Pages of Library Journal." <u>Library Journal</u>, 1996: 56-72.

Holzberlein, Deanne B. "Dewey Decimal Classification." <u>The World Book Encyclopedia</u>. 1990 ed.

"Melvil Dewey, Founder, Library Bureau." 4 Oct.1998 <http://www.librarybureau.com/melvil.html>.

From *Practical Steps to the Research Process for High School* © 1999 Libraries Unlimited. 800-237-6124.

LMT: Looking at the Research Checklist reminds me that if some of you have not yet come to the LMC to pre-search for specific subtopics, you *must* use general ones from the Research Process sheet for today's activity. You absolutely cannot go on with your research without subtopics, or as we said before, you have no idea what you're doing! If you wrote subtopics in the form of questions, then take a minute and circle the keyword in each one. What I'm leading to is that subtopics act as the title of your note pages. Therefore, they each should be only one or two words.

On the overhead, I still have general subtopics filled in from our first day. We'll use these to prepare sample notetaking sheets today. Take the first blank sheet of notebook paper, and centered at the top, write your first subtopic. (The LMT places a clear transparency on the overhead and writes the first subtopic from *Figure 8-8*.) I strongly encourage you to use pencil. That way you can erase if you change your mind later.

It should be obvious what to do next. Take the second note page and record the second subtopic. I'll give you a couple of minutes to continue through all five subtopics. (LMT circulates through the class to do a spot check.) Bring these prepared note sheets with you every day that you are scheduled for research.

Student Activity B: Recording Notes

LMT writes on Figure 8-9 in the manner indicated on Figure 8-10.

LMT: Let's practice recording some notes. How can we do that when we haven't started looking for information yet? I'll show you. Be patient with me while I flip back and forth between the overhead examples we have seen before and new ones we will create today. When you do research you will have all five of the subtopic note sheets. Spread them out like a fan on the table in front of you so that you can grab the one you need at any time. Got the picture?

To begin, let's look at the Final Bibliography overhead example (*Figure 8-9*). Are we putting the cart before the horse? I know you will not have a bibliography that looks like this your first day of research! We do not expect a complete, typed, alphabetized list like this until the very end of your project. What you will create instead is a rough bibliography. (LMT places *Figure 8-10* on the overhead projector.) What makes this rough?

Student: It's not in alphabetical order. But you said we didn't need numbers.

LMT: Right! It is not necessary to number bibliography entries unless you have more than a page of them. Now I am going to tell you something that seems the opposite, but I guarantee you will understand in a minute. Let's pretend it is tomorrow. You come in to begin research. All the computers are full so you get an encyclopedia. That's the best, easiest place to start anyway. Here it is on this Rough Bibliography sheet. (LMT points out the reference entry on *Figure 8-10*.) It's the first source this student used; that's why it's labeled one.

Let's say the encyclopedia has good information that matches your subtopic, "What" (*Figure 8-11*), so also write a number one in the left margin of the "What" note page to identify these first few notes. Do you see that you are giving yourself a code and a time-saving strategy? As you skim through the text, with your pencil down, facts jump out at you, and as you record them on the corresponding note page (LMT demonstrates recording notes by "Greeking" lines on a blank "What" overhead), you are identifying the source they came from.

Fig. 8-10. Teaching Model:
Rough Bibliography

Rough Bibliography

(1) Holzberlein, Deanne B. "Dewey Decimal Classification." <u>The World Book Encyclopedia</u>. 1990 ed.

(2) "Dewey, Melvil." <u>Microsoft Encarta '98 Encyclopedia</u>. CD-ROM, 1998 ed.

(3) "Melvil Dewey, Founder, Library Bureau." 4 Oct. 1998 <http://www.librarybureau.com/melvil.html>.

(4) Dewey, Melvil. <u>Dewey Decimal Classification and Relative Index</u>. New York: Forest Press, Inc. 1958.

(5) Ferguson, Anna Marie. "Historical Highlights from the Pages of <u>Library Journal</u>." Library Journal, 1996: 56-72.

From *Practical Steps to the Research Process for High School* © 1999 Libraries Unlimited. 800-237-6124.

Fig. 8-11. Teaching Model:
Notebook Paper Setup

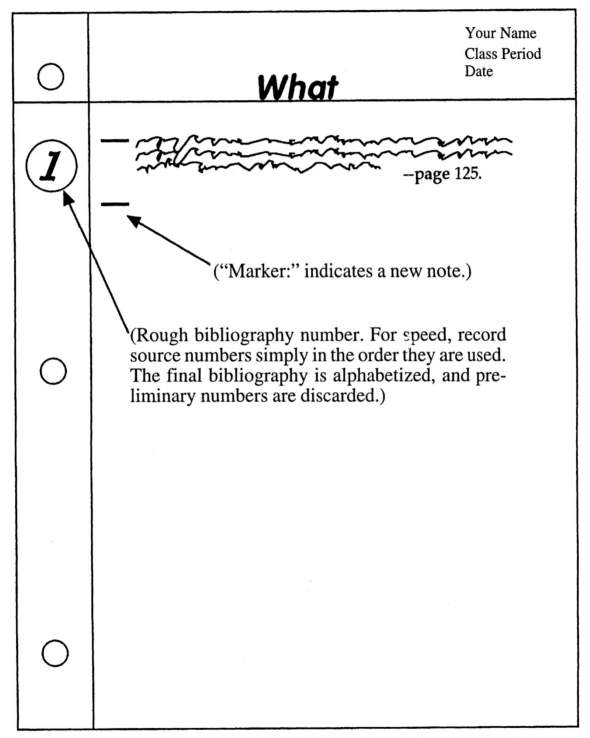

From *Practical Steps to the Research Process for High School* © 1999 Libraries Unlimited. 800-237-6124.

Literacy

Technology Proficiency

LMT: As you read further in this source, you see there is information for the "Where" note page (not shown in this lesson). Remember, all your subtopic note pages are spread out in front of you. Grab the "Where" page, and again record a number one in the left margin because you are still using your first source. Record the good notes you find. (LMT repeats the "Greeking" and bibliography number one on a "Where" transparency.) Continue reading, evaluating, and recording notes for 10 to 20 notes. Let's review that the number one on the rough bibliography number matches to the number one on any of the five subtopic sheets where you recorded information from this source. Makes life easy, huh?

Student: But why did you say stop at 10 to 20 notes if there's plenty of information in that book?

LMT: Great question! Remember that a report cannot come from only one source? You must force yourself to move to another source so that you fulfill the requirement of using at least three formats and five sources of information. This is also a way of forcing you to see that different sources also have lots of great information, whereas you might have only stopped at one or two!

Well, the bell rings. You come back the next day and are able to get on a computer where you find a good CD-ROM article (indicated as number two on *Figure 8-10*). On your rough bibliography you continue to accurately record bibliography entries numbered simply in the order in which you use them. A helpful strategy to remember is to record bibliography information *before* you begin notetaking, on the day you first use the source. Don't take a chance on thinking you can do it later. There is no guarantee the same source, particularly a nonfiction book, will be here later when you need it. Follow a good business rule:

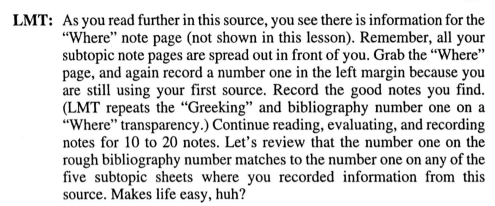

To be efficient, handle something only once!

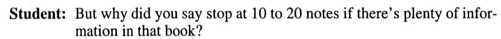

On each day of research, repeat the procedure just demonstrated until you end up with several pages of good notes on each subtopic, as this student had done (refer back to *Figure 8-7*). At the end of your research, you'll reorganize the rough bibliography into alphabetical order and type it up as a final bibliography (*Figure 8-9*).

Fig. 8-12. General Notetaking Instructions

- **Locate** one good source each day, and don't waste time looking for other things.

- **Prepare** your note cards/sheets, each titled with a subtopic.

- **Record** MLA bibliography information for each source on a "rough" bibliography page before you begin notetaking.

- **Identify** notes with a source number to accurately cite the source of information.

- **Use** reading strategies—"chunk" text, pencil down, skim and scan—to locate information that matches your subtopics.

- **Use** evaluating strategies: match information to topic and subtopics. Skip the rest unless you add subtopics.

- **Use** notetaking strategies: important keyword facts; no small words; no sentences without footnotes or endnotes. Aim for a minimum of 10-15 notes per subtopic.

From *Practical Steps to the Research Process for High School* © 1999 Libraries Unlimited. 800-237-6124.

Alternative Teaching: Note Card Notetaking

Timing: 20 minutes. Do not teach both note card and notebook paper notetaking strategies at the same time.

Concepts for Using Note Cards

It is important to include an alternate section on notetaking with note cards for the high school level. I strongly believe that using note cards should be the first method taught in Research Process instruction.

Important Idea

> *The purpose in using cards is not to teach a system or a methodology of recording information as much as it is to teach students how to think! There is a sequential logic to note card notetaking that, once learned, becomes a permanent part of the student's information management skills.*

The Rationale for Note Cards

Information Literacy

In my experience, cards for notetaking can and should be used from grades three to nine. I have used them as early as first grade, and some high school teachers prefer tenth to twelfth grade students to use them if there has been no previous instruction in notetaking. Whether or not they've had middle school training, I believe all incoming ninth graders should have a note-card-based research project. That evens out the playing field and prepares all students equally for the tougher expectations of information management in later grades. *Figure 8-13* represents a template of blank note cards which I use with students who are afraid of losing lots of individual cards. During research, these attached cards are titled with subtopics, used for recording keyword notes, and they are cut apart for the final Research Process step of sorting and numbering notes.

The Rationale for Notebook Paper Notes

Lifelong Skills

When teaching high school students, I have adjusted notetaking instruction away from note cards in direct response to the needs of the teachers with whom I collaborate, and to the needs of higher-grade students. Once students have information management skills in place, there seems to be a plateau where they do not want to be bothered anymore with shuffling cards. My response was the creation of notebook paper strategies, which I use almost exclusively in high school collaborative research lessons. In my experience, juniors and seniors need a notetaking model that enables a smoother transition to the independent work they do in late high school and college.

Fig. 8-13. Template of Student Note Cards

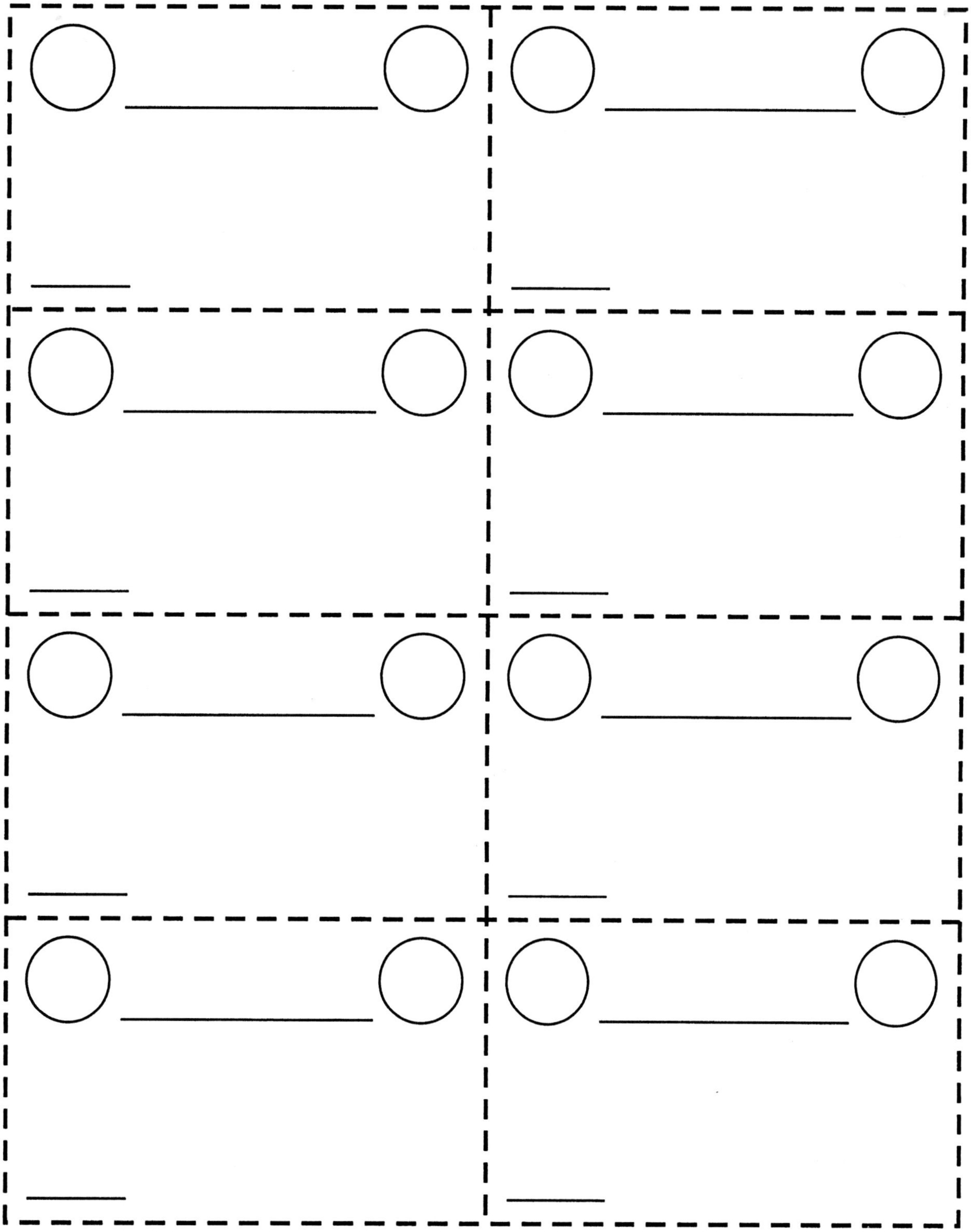

From *Practical Steps to the Research Process for High School* © 1999 Libraries Unlimited. 800-237-6124.

Concepts to Deter Plagiarism

Electronic Sources

Students must be actively involved in information gathering instead of passively receiving information from electronic sources. Discourage students from electronically copying and pasting information. Instead, instruct that electronic printouts should be highlighted to select keyword facts which are then hand recorded on cards or notebook paper. Teachers: collect notes! That is the only way to validate genuine notetaking.

Subtopics

Subtopics both control information gathering and are controlled by the information found. Subtopics enable students to know what information to select and what to skip, thereby preventing wholesale copying. Whether specific or general, allow students the freedom to change subtopics at any time.

Why Notes?

Keyword notetaking totally eliminates direct copying. Paraphrasing and summarizing are also legitimate information gathering skills. It is perhaps due to lack of any notetaking instruction that students may resort to copying from sources. Notetaking must be taught, then practiced.

Concepts for Information Ownership

Important Idea

The dominant concept in this section is that genuine notetaking is the key to information ownership. This is a process skill that enables students to learn how to learn.

Lifelong Skills

The mental act of notetaking is transferring information from the source and processing (reducing) its original form into notes to create ownership. The resulting "shrinky dink" notes are expanded by prior knowledge and creativity into good writing. When information is plagiarized, no learning occurs because information is not processed by critical evaluation but is merely repeated in its original form.

The physical act of notetaking is the recording of information using specific strategies to enable both speed and accuracy. The repetition of useful strategies creates skills for lifelong learning.

Information ownership is also created by 1) critically selecting (analyzing) information; 2) changing the order in which information originally appears; and 3) combining (synthesizing) information thoughtfully from a variety of sources.

Concepts for Copied Notes

The student notetaking example in *Figure 8-16* is an example of note card notes that look more like copying than real notetaking, similar to *Figure 8-4*. This lesson involves discussion and demonstration of whether the recorded information in *Figure 8-16* supports the subtopic. Discuss improvements with the class.

Concepts for Good Notes

Notes need to *look* like notes! Use *Figure 8-19* to point out the reasons this is good note form: no beginning capital letter or ending period, basic keywords recorded with a minimum of small, unnecessary words.

Teachers never have to read student notes. However, point out to students that having one note on a card makes it obvious to teachers, by merely glancing at note cards, if information has been copied.

Contrast the cards in *Figure 8-16* with *Figure 8-17* to discuss times when full, longer sentences are or are not permissible. For example, the student's notes in *Figure 8-16* show quotation marks and a page citation to indicate that this is intended to be a copied, documented quotation. That's perfectly alright. However, the LMT should slide down the overhead to the bottom card to show that it is the same! In fact, every single note this student did is the same, which is not alright. She was simply copying!

Don't forget to identify the strategies of paraphrasing and summarizing as legitimate notetaking techniques, although time does not permit the teaching of these strategies in this notetaking lesson. Instead, they are supplemental to the focus in this guide book on researching with facts and keyword notes.

Concepts for Making a Bad Note Good

Using the blank note card template (*Figure 8-18*), the LMT copies the bad sentence example from the top note card in *Figure 8-16* and demonstrates techniques for changing a "bad" note into a good note by:

- Eliminating the obvious marks of a sentence: the capital letter at the beginning and the period at the end.

- Crossing out small, unnecessary words such as *a*, *an*, and *the* and replacing them with commas or dashes.

- Stressing that notes should be *new* information. Never repeat obvious or prior knowledge. Show students never to repeat the topic or subtopics on a note card.

Problem Solving

Literacy

Concepts for Judging the Content of Good Notes

The simple criteria for a good note is that it produces good writing! Read aloud to the class the keyword fact created in the previous demonstration. Be quite dramatic in transforming it into an accurate but creative sentence by embellishing the keywords with juicy adjectives and interesting prior knowledge to produce one or more fluent, knowledge-based sentences.

This keyword note:
"autumn 1919 —attend meetings —small nationalist group —German Workers' Party"

Becomes this sentence:
"By the autumn of 1919, young Adolf Hitler began to attend meetings of a small nationalist group called the German Workers' Party, where he could express his growing socialist ideas."

Lifelong Skills

On a more practical basis, emphasize that an important aspect of good keyword notetaking is speed. The student laboriously copying out of a book is quickly bypassed by the student with effective notetaking strategies who uses more sources to gather more information in far less time.

Instructor Preparation for Note Card Notetaking

Reasonable Expectations

Students first count out 10 precut cards from the bins in the middle of each table. This represents the number of notes an average student can be reasonably expected to complete in one class period. Keep in mind this includes locating a source, reading and comprehending the information, and evaluating, selecting, and recording notes. Advanced students are expected to take more than 10 notes per day. Special students will take fewer.

- The number of subtopics, five in this case, can be a guide for a reasonable number of research days spent in the LMC. Five days for five subtopics.

- The minimum number of notes, 10 in this case, multiplied by the number of days spent in the LMC equals a reasonable amount of total notes which are expected to be successfully completed. The goal here is 50 notes for five days of hands-on research.

- The minimum number of notes can also be a guide for a reasonable expectation of the number of pages the student later writes. Ten good notes should equal at least a page, or more, of writing. The final research paper should therefore be at least five pages in length. Setting practical expectations results in greater student success.

Fig. 8-14. Note Card Setup

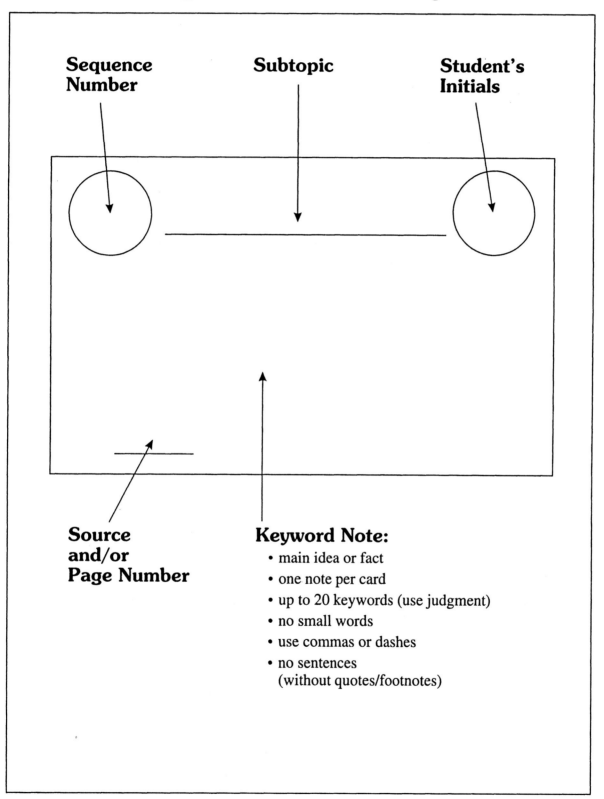

From *Practical Steps to the Research Process for High School* © 1999 Libraries Unlimited. 800-237-6124.

Preparing the Note Cards

Following the notetaking lesson, students prepare the note cards that will be used the next day in hands-on research. Using *Figure 8-14*, the LMT demonstrates the following directions.

- Student's initials go in the upper right area of blank note cards.

- For the purpose of this demonstration, title two note cards with each of the five subtopics, for a total of 10 cards. Eventually, students will have 10 cards titled with each of the five subtopics, for a total of 50 cards.

- Leave the upper left area of the card blank. It will be used for the note's sequence number during the sorting step of the process.

- Demonstrate how to use the line in the lower left of the card to cite the note's source matching the rough bibliography (see *Figure 8-10*). Include the page number for a quotation. Remind students the final bibliography (see *Figure 8-9*) is alphabetized.

Fig. 8-15. Sample Note Card

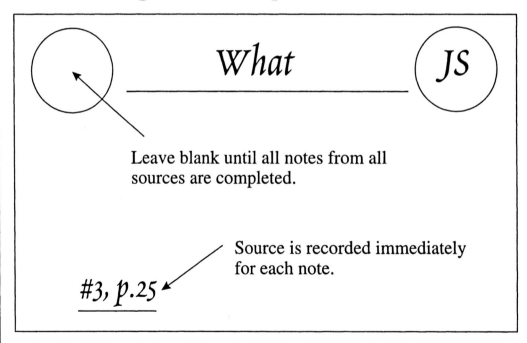

From *Practical Steps to the Research Process for High School* © 1999 Libraries Unlimited. 800-237-6124.

Student Lesson: Note Card Notetaking

Getting Started

The following incomplete script addresses only those additions or changes to the script for notebook paper notes which pertain specifically to note card notetaking.

LMT: Let's take a minute to make sure each of you has cards which we'll use for today's notetaking activity. In the middle of your table is a small box filled with cards. This is how we recycle here in the LMC. Some of them are old card catalog cards. Remember those ancient things? But most of it is recycled paper from the computer printers or copy machine. In lower grades I often give out sheets of prepared note cards (*Figure 8-13*), but you'll easily be able to make your own cards.

Count out 10 cards. Why 10? That will be the goal for each day's notetaking. You're scheduled for a total of five days in the LMC for research. Five times 10 equals 50. Dig out your Research Checklist (*Figure 8-8*), and in the "Read and Notetake" section, write "50" in the blank space after letter B. Is everyone clear that this is *minimum* number of notes expected?

Can you take more than ten cards per subtopic when you start your own research? Of course you can! But only after you have completed 10 notes for every subtopic. Also, switch sources after 10 notes to pace yourself. After 50 notes, take all you want, where you want! There is an unending supply of note cards available here in the library media center. You never have to buy index cards, unless you prefer them.

Copied Notes

LMT: This is a very powerful example (*Figure 8-4*) of a student who honestly thought he was taking notes. He was a senior! I did not get upset with him about copying because when I asked, he said no one had ever showed him what notetaking was! Using note cards, instead of notebook paper, is one way to prevent this mass confusion of unorganized and undifferentiated information. Here is an example of student note cards. (LMT puts *Figure 8-16* onto the overhead.) What do you think?

Fig. 8-16. Copied Notes

"World War II," <u>*World Book Encyclopedia*</u>, *Volume 9, 1990.*

"In the autumn of 1919, he began to attend meetings of a small nationalist group called the German Workers' Party. He joined the party and changed its name to the National Socialist German Workers' Party." pg. 254

"World War II," <u>*World Book Encyclopedia*</u>, *Volume 9, 1990.*

"The party he joined became known as the Nazi Party. The Nazis called for the union into one nation of all Germans, including the Austrians and German minorities in Czechoslovakia and other countries." pg. 254

From *Practical Steps to the Research Process for High School* © 1999 Libraries Unlimited. 800-237-6124.

LMT: Can anyone compare these cards (*Figure 8-16*) to the page of note-taking we just saw? (*Figure 8-4*)

Student: They've both copied sentences, but I see quotation marks here.

LMT: Yes. At least this student is giving credit, the point of yesterday's lesson. But almost every one of this student's cards looked just like this. So are they *really* notetaking? Are they *thinking* about their information? I must also remind you that if a teacher does not teach you about endnotes or footnotes and does not require them for a project, then there shouldn't be any quotation marks anywhere in your notes. If there are no quotation marks, and no footnotes, that means you *cannot* copy even one sentence for this project. Do you get my meaning?

So we're back to square one. We need to learn to make notes! Let's take a minute to read through the items on the Research Process guide sheet (*Figure 8-1*) to see if these notes (*Figure 8-16*) fit the criteria. Letter A says, "One note per card! Title cards with subtopics." Cards are really great because they instantly identify separate pieces of information. You never have the confusion of masses of information stuck together like we just saw (*Figure 8-4*) and like you may be used to doing when you use notebook paper.

Letter C goes on to say, "Record only important facts or keywords," which I think we've just decided this person hasn't done. She's picked everything and tried to get away with it by using quotation marks. Let's try another example.

Notes Should Look Like Notes

LMT: This looks better! (LMT puts *Figure 8-17* onto the overhead.) Compared to the note cards we just saw, let's pick this apart and see how these notes measure up to the strategies listed on the Research Process sheet. Any ideas?

Student: No capital letter or period, so it doesn't look like a sentence.

Student: It definitely looks more like a keyword fact, but I still see verbs and small words, like *and*, and *at*.

Fig. 8-17. Better Note Cards

> *conditions*   *JT*
>
> *people died from starvation, sickness and epidemics not from being battered to death*
>
> *#6 / pg. 24*

> *conditions*   *JT*
>
> *over 2 1/2 million people were executed at Auschwitz and 500,000 more starved to death*
>
> *#2 / pg. 89*

From *Practical Steps to the Research Process for High School* © 1999 Libraries Unlimited. 800-237-6124.

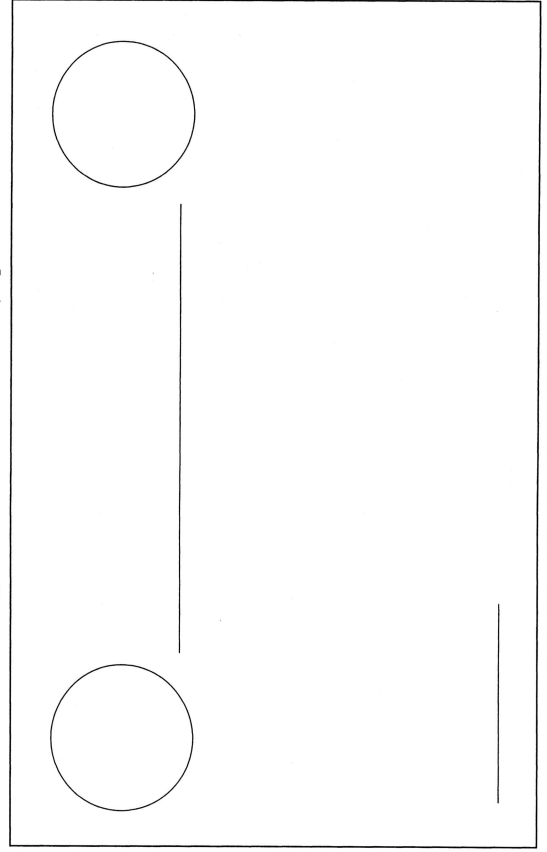

Fig. 8-18. Blank Note Card Template

From *Practical Steps to the Research Process for High School* © 1999 Libraries Unlimited. 800-237-6124.

LMT: Great! You are already beginning to do a better job of critically evaluating information. You're recognizing strategies that will terrifically speed up your own notetaking. Shall we try to construct a better note?

Making a Bad Note Good

LMT: We're going to look at the rest of the items on the Research Process sheet by doing an activity with this blank card (*Figure 8-18*). First, let's copy onto it the first sentence from our bad note cards (*Figure 8-16*). Should I even bother copying the second sentence?

Student: No. The sheet says to only put one note on a card.

LMT: Good. Remember: new note, new card. If you run out of cards, I always have tons available. Are you making a connection here with the requirements for this project? Ten notes a day for you will be easy partly due to the one note per card rule. Let's tackle some other strategies.

Here's what this note says: "In the autumn of 1919, he began to attend meetings of a small nationalist group called the German Workers' Party." The first obvious change comes from letter E on your Research Process sheet. It says, "No sentences!" unless you use quotes, which she has, but she's quoted everything! Let's cross out the quotes and show some notetaking strategies to change it into a keyword fact.

How do you make a good note? Letter D says to "Discard small words like *a*, *an*, and *the*. Use commas or dashes instead." Let's try that. First cross out "In the" They're not necessary, nor is the word "he" because it refers to the topic! Remember, never, ever, ever repeat your topic in your notes! Why would you waste valuable library time repeating something you already know? What *should* a note include? New information only! Only write down stuff your brain has never heard of before. Later on when you write, you are supposed to combine new notes with information you already know. That is called learning!

Let's continue on and the next thing we can cross out is "of a." Your brain will automatically fill in all these little words when you write.

Can you see the enormous amount of time this person wasted copying stuff she already knew? Let's especially cross out "called the." Including the verb in the note automatically makes it a sentence. Let's read back what we have left and see if it makes sense (LMT reads the keyword note in its new form, seen in *Figure 8-17*.)

Fig. 8-19. Bad Note Changed to Good Note

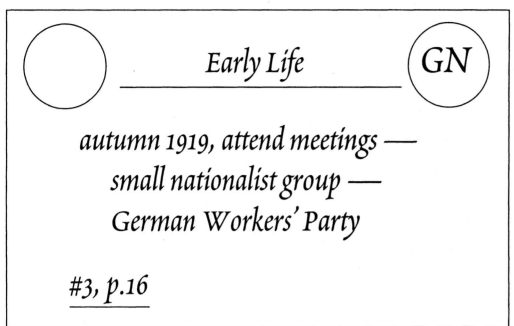

From *Practical Steps to the Research Process for High School* © 1999 Libraries Unlimited. 800-237-6124.

The Purpose of Good Notes

Expand on this brief reminder using the concepts listed in the instructor information section.

LMT: This isn't even my note, but it makes sense to me. What is the purpose of a note? To make a sentence, and not just one sentence. With more practice in notetaking, you should be able to write quite a bit from a really excellent keyword note.

That's an easy thing to do here. (LMT role models a sentence.) When you write your paper, expand on the keyword note information with prior knowledge, with recently read but unrecorded related information, and with what I call "accurate adjectives." A note is only as good as the memory it evokes.

Chapter 9

*Sorting and
Numbering Notes:
Lesson 3, Part 3*

Instructor

Student Lesson

"This makes writing really easy!"
—Surprised student

147

Fig. 9-1. Research Process: Sort and Number Notes

Topic
A. Locate topic ideas in grade-level texts, unit concepts, current literature studies.
B. Check in the library media center for sources to determine supporting information.
C. Cross-check in an encyclopedia to narrow or broaden a topic.
D. Create a thesis statement to investigate the topic.

Subtopics
A. Ask yourself: What do I want to know about my topic?
B. Specific: Pre-search encyclopedia or nonfiction book's table of contents for ideas.
C. General:
    Thing: who, what, when, where, why/how.
    Person: early life, education, accomplishments, later life.
D. Minimum of three subtopics, maximum is determined by time and information.
E. List subtopics in outline form by Roman numeral. Construct outline guide.

Sources
A. Source: anything used for information.
    Format of sources:
        Print: books, references, magazines, newspapers, maps, charts, etc.
        Nonprint: videos, software, CD-ROMs, Internet.
B. Number of formats (minimum of three). Number of sources.
C. Credit sources using an official guide such as the MLA Bibliography sheet.
D. Know the difference:
    Primary vs. secondary sources.
    Regular vs. annotated bibliography.

Read/Think/Select
A. Read an entire "chunk" *before* selecting facts. Put your pencil down!
B. Think about what was read. What was important?
C. Select appropriate information from each "chunk."

Notetake
A. Note cards: One note per card! Title cards with subtopics.
B. Notebook Paper: Bullet or mark each note. Do not number notes at this time.
C. Record only important facts or keywords.
D. Discard small words like *a*, *an*, and *the*. Use commas and dashes instead.
E. No sentences!
F. Use quotation marks when copying. Give credit with source and page number.
G. Alternative information gathering includes paraphrasing or summarizing.

Sort and Number Notes
A. Sort notes by subtopic, by paragraph ideas, and then by supporting details (outline).
B. Read all your notes. Select good notes; discard irrelevant notes.
C. Sequence notes for fluent writing.
D. Number all notes consecutively from section to section.

Extension
    Write/Publish/Present
    Final bibliography
    Technology integration

Evaluation

From *Practical Steps to the Research Process for High School* © 1999 Libraries Unlimited. 800-237-6124.

Chapter Concepts

Reading Notes

It is only at the end of notetaking that students get a global picture of the information they have found. Besides promoting literacy, re-reading their own notes promotes process writing through the prewriting (or motivational) step preceding composing. Reading notes strengthens students' ties to prior knowledge and to recently read new information.

What's So Important About Sorting Notes?

Sorting notes finalizes the outline for writing which was initiated with the selection of subtopics. The labeling of notes with subtopics made them initially self-sorting. However, students must still make important decisions about selecting and sequencing their notes in order to prepare for writing. This step continues the evaluation stage of the information literacy sequence which began with the reading and notetaking steps. Indeed, the sorting strategies after notetaking are almost the same as the critical reading of sources before notetaking.

Evaluation and interpretation of notes increases ownership of information. Redundancy, irrelevancy, even missing pieces become apparent. Personal reflection promotes personal growth in knowledge of the topic and validates research strategies that were either used well or could be strengthened. Research novices should probably sort notes into subtopics, identified with Roman numerals, to create the paper's outline of information. Notes can be further sorted into subsections, even paragraphs. Sorting notes is a personal decision.

Numbering Notes

Numbering notes comes last! Notes should be numbered consecutively from subtopic section to section, never starting over at number one. One stack of consecutively numbered note cards equals a report that simply writes itself!

Instructor Information

Getting Started

It is important to note that the Research Process ends with the end of research. This is the final lesson before students begin their own individual research. Put *Figure 9-2* on the overhead, and review the strategies for recording notes on notebook paper to create a smooth transition to sorting notes.

- *With subtopics as a title for notes, the information students record from every source is automatically sorted.*

- *Notes which are coded with the source from which they came confirm for the teacher that the required sources were indeed used. Identifying sources on notes also provides an efficient system for students if they need to create footnotes or endnotes later.*

- *From the clearly visible content and abbreviated form of notes, it is easy for the student (and teacher) to see that good notetaking strategies have occurred, creating ownership of the information.*

- *Notes that look like notes and are clearly marked and differentiated are much easier to read, make sense of, and sort than notes which are unmarked.*

- *The clear separation of notes makes counting notes a snap. This is important because in order to write a balanced report, a minimum number of notes needs to be gathered for each subtopic. A balanced number of notes easily converts into a balanced outline to prepare for writing a report which covers the required content in a meaningful way.*

Reading Notes

Critical reading produces better notes, which must in turn be read critically. The experienced research teacher knows that students do not take perfect notes the first time around or even the second time. Whether you have younger or less experienced students using note cards or older students using notebook paper, reading to notetake is a skill which definitely improves with age and practice, but all students make progress when they re-read their own notes! With the return to original information cut off, and the goal of good writing now facing them, reading their own notes triggers a sequence of criticism and evaluation during which students recognize the quality and quantity of information they have gathered. "I know something I need to go back and get," is a comment you'll often hear. "That's okay. Work with what you have. You'll do better next time," replies the teacher or LMT.

The tie-in to literacy is obvious as the student continues to bond with their new information in order to evaluate it for sorting. (Title I and ELL teachers just love this!) The reading of their own notes is important to the student, not only to review their work, but to connect to prior or newly acquired knowledge. This is learning!

Thinking About, Selecting, and Sequencing Notes

Critical thinking about notes is a natural consequence of critically reading notes. The instructor knows reading notes jogs memory and causes the student to ponder their information. Students may realize they don't like some of the things they have recorded or realize they've left some important items out. Critical thinking continues as the student evaluates which notes to include or exclude and then which comes first, second, and third. Almost inadvertently, what is occurring is the transformation of information into knowledge as the student digests the content-area material.

Numbering Notes

Figure 9-3 for notebook paper notes and *Figure 9-4* for note card notes show how to number notes consecutively. Relevancy is provided with the example of asking students to remember how they connected dots when they were little. Out of the numbered notes pops a section of their final paper which practically writes itself. It is clear that they have just connected the dots! "Wow! If I'd only known this when *I* was a kid!" says the classroom teacher.

Literacy

ELL/Special Modifications

Problem Solving

Content-Area Standard

Fig. 9-2. Teaching Model: Notebook Paper Notes

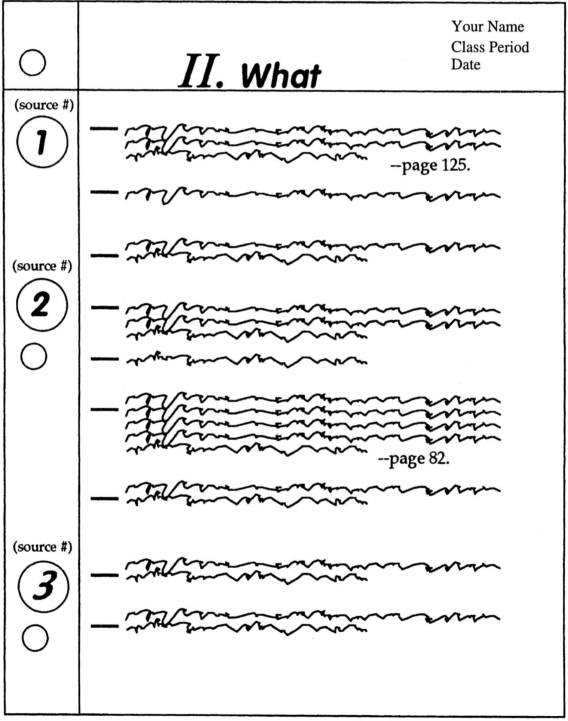

From *Practical Steps to the Research Process for High School* © 1999 Libraries Unlimited. 800-237-6124.

Student Lesson: Sorting and Numbering Notebook Paper Notes

Timimg: 10 minutes.

Reading Notes

Literacy

LMT: The strategies you used for recording notes (*Figure 9-2*) make it a snap to complete the final step of sorting and sequencing your notes. First, put all of your notetaking sheets, by subtopic, in front of you. Scan the notes quickly to see which entire section you would like to discuss first. For example, if you want your "What" notes to be the first section of your paper, put a Roman numeral one at the top of each "What" note sheet. If you want to discuss the "Where" notes next, write Roman numeral two at the top. You are creating a working outline for your rough draft. When you have finished all of the sections, stack them back up in outline order. This order either matches or rearranges your original outline for subtopics on your Student Checklist.

Take the first Roman numeral section off the stack. As it says on the Research Process sheet, you must now read your notes. Do you know I once had a student raise his hand while he was reading his notes and say, "Can you tell me what this says?" I looked at him for a few seconds because I couldn't believe he was really asking me that! "Whose notes are they?" I asked. "Oh, yeah," he said with a big blush.

Thinking About and Sorting Notes

Problem Solving

LMT: Reading all your notes together enables you to make judgments about your information. A note that looked great five days ago may now be irrelevant or repetitious compared to what you found later in other sources. As you read, cross out the notes that no longer work. In other words, "de-select" them.

After you've selected the useful notes in the first section, the Research Process sheet says to sort them in several ways. We have already grouped them by subtopic, so you need to prioritize them in some logical order. This order is completely subjective. It could be by time, by an order of reasoning out a point, or just by what makes the best sense. It's even easy using this method to establish paragraph main ideas and sort the supporting details.

Fig. 9-3. Teaching Model:
Numbering Notebook Paper Notes

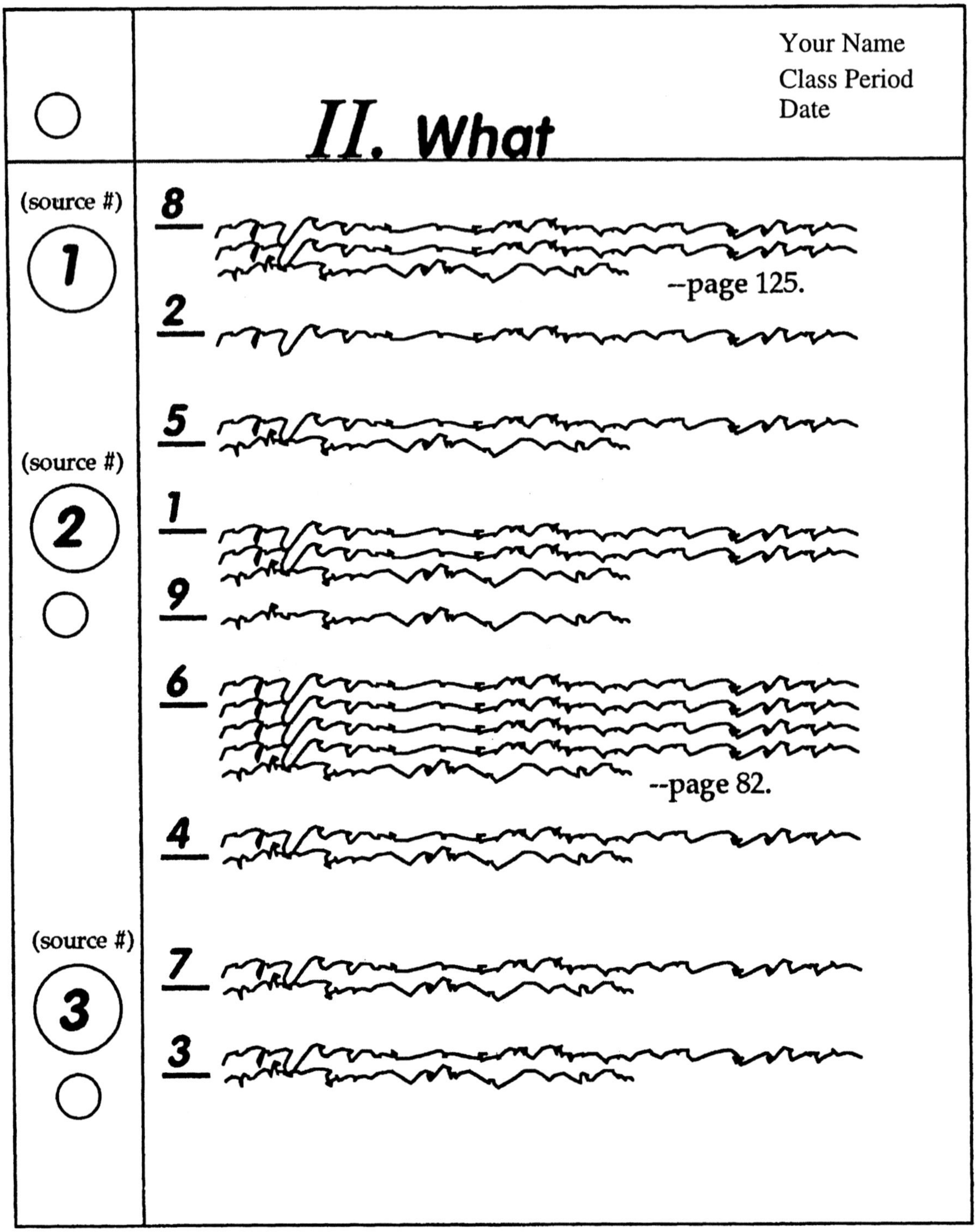

Your Name
Class Period
Date

II. What

(source #)
1

8
⎯⎯⎯⎯⎯⎯⎯⎯⎯⎯⎯⎯⎯⎯⎯⎯⎯⎯⎯
--page 125.

2
⎯⎯⎯⎯⎯⎯⎯⎯⎯⎯⎯⎯⎯⎯⎯⎯⎯⎯⎯

5
⎯⎯⎯⎯⎯⎯⎯⎯⎯⎯⎯⎯⎯⎯⎯⎯⎯⎯⎯

(source #)
2

1
⎯⎯⎯⎯⎯⎯⎯⎯⎯⎯⎯⎯⎯⎯⎯⎯⎯⎯⎯

9
⎯⎯⎯⎯⎯⎯⎯⎯⎯⎯⎯⎯⎯⎯⎯⎯⎯⎯⎯

6
⎯⎯⎯⎯⎯⎯⎯⎯⎯⎯⎯⎯⎯⎯⎯⎯⎯⎯⎯
--page 82.

4
⎯⎯⎯⎯⎯⎯⎯⎯⎯⎯⎯⎯⎯⎯⎯⎯⎯⎯⎯

(source #)
3

7
⎯⎯⎯⎯⎯⎯⎯⎯⎯⎯⎯⎯⎯⎯⎯⎯⎯⎯⎯

3
⎯⎯⎯⎯⎯⎯⎯⎯⎯⎯⎯⎯⎯⎯⎯⎯⎯⎯⎯

From *Practical Steps to the Research Process for High School* © 1999 Libraries Unlimited. 800-237-6124.

Numbering Notes

LMT: The very last thing you do is number the notes. You were told earlier to never number notes *during* notetaking because you hadn't gathered all of your information yet. Something you may have numbered as one at first has very little chance of being the first fact discussed in that section of your paper. Does this make sense?

Student: Yes, but what about the other pages of notes?

LMT: Good question. Deal with only one subtopic section of your paper at a time and assign numbers to all the notes in that set. Repeat this system section by section for all five subtopics with one important change. When you start section two, do you start the first note you select with number one again? No! Continue numbering all notes in consecutive order. If the last note in section one was number 18, the first note in section two will be number 19.

Do you have to do this exact system forever? No. Come up with a system of your own for *what* to do! This is teaching you *how* to think about sorting information.

When you have worked your way through all five sections, all of the information for an entire term paper is completely sorted and numbered in final order. Remember when you were a little kid doing "connect-the-dot" puzzles, and out of all those dots appeared an animal? Well, out of this comes a fully written term paper. It's a miracle! When kids who don't know how to do this are sitting there, completely frustrated and overwhelmed, with a few books open in front of them and a paper due tomorrow, you will be sitting there with a paper that's basically already written! Here is the formula:

Numbered notes
Prior knowledge
+ Creative brain

Best-ever project and learning!

Fig. 9-4. Teaching Model: Sorting Note Cards

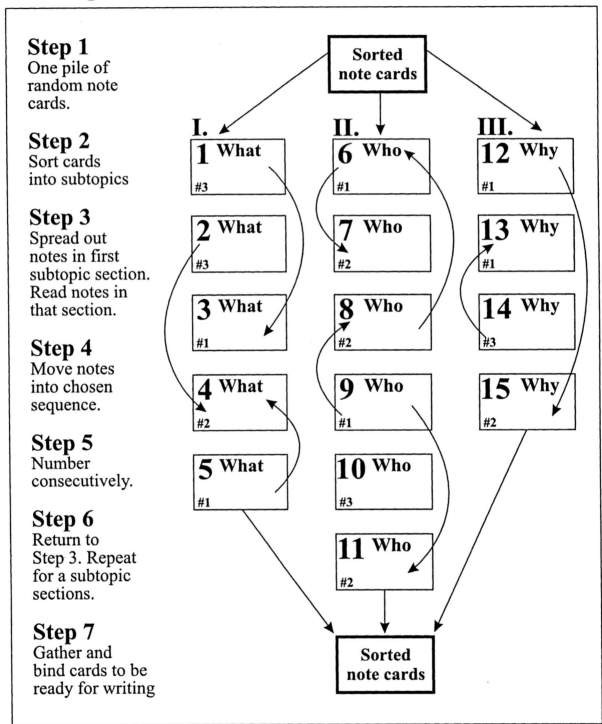

Step 1
One pile of random note cards.

Step 2
Sort cards into subtopics

Step 3
Spread out notes in first subtopic section. Read notes in that section.

Step 4
Move notes into chosen sequence.

Step 5
Number consecutively.

Step 6
Return to Step 3. Repeat for a subtopic sections.

Step 7
Gather and bind cards to be ready for writing

Sorted note cards

I.

1 What	#3
2 What	#3
3 What	#1
4 What	#2
5 What	#1

II.

6 Who	#1
7 Who	#2
8 Who	#2
9 Who	#1
10 Who	#3
11 Who	#2

III.

12 Why	#1
13 Why	#1
14 Why	#3
15 Why	#2

Sorted note cards

From *Practical Steps to the Research Process for High School* © 1999 Libraries Unlimited. 800-237-6124.

Student Lesson: Sorting and Numbering Note Card Notes

Lifelong Skills

Information Literacy

Timing: 10 minutes. At least the first time this activity is done, it should be done under teacher or library media teacher direction. See Figure 9-4 to follow these steps.

Step 1: Gather

Have one pile of random note cards which have been checked for quantity and quality by the classroom teacher. The teacher does not have to *read* them but quickly reviews students' notes. (Reading, notetaking, and recording strategies should be apparent.)

Step 2: Sort

Sort cards first by subtopic. Decide which subtopic is to be addressed first in the written paper. On the Student Checklist (*Figure 8-7*), label it with Roman numeral one. Continue to prioritize and label the remaining subtopic sections with Roman numerals to form the final writing outline. Sort all note cards into each section, but the cards themselves do not need to be individually labeled with Roman numerals.

Step 3: Read

Select the first stack, and place the other stacks at a distance to enable work space. On the table, spread out all cards from this stack. Read all of the cards.

Step 4: Sequence

De-select (toss out) notes which are repetitive or irrelevant. Prioritize note cards by physically placing them in the order in which the facts make sense by sorting, grouping, and sequencing cards using subjective logic such as time, logical steps in the construction of a thing or idea, paragraph main ideas, and supporting details.

Re-read all cards after sequencing. "Tell" yourself, or a partner, the report by flipping from card to card. "If you can speak it, you can write it," reminds the LMT. Does it make sense? Make additional card placement adjustments.

Step 5: Number

Number the cards in the upper left area indicated with a circle on the Note Card Setup (*Figure 8-18*). Pick up the cards from the first section in number order and set the stack aside.

Step 6: Repeat

Repeat steps three to five for each subtopic stack of cards with one important difference. Do *not* start with number one for the first note card in each section. Number notes consecutively throughout all subtopic sections. For example, if the last card in the first stack was number 18, the first card in the second stack will be number 19.

Step 7: Gather

Unless the stack is prohibitively thick, place all notecards in one final stack, numbered consecutively. Rubber band them together or place stack in a zip lock bag. You are ready to write, or rather, the paper is ready to write itself!

Section 3

Application and Accountability

Chapter 10
Hands-on Research

Chapter 11
Tracking and Evaluation

Chapter 12
Writing the Rough Draft

159

Chapter 10

Hands-on Research

Instructor

Student Lesson

"I'm ready, I'm ready!"
—Student actually anxious
to start research!

Fig. 10-1. Dewey Decimal System

000-General Works
000 Monsters, Computers
010 Bibliographies
020 Libraries
030 Encyclopedias
050 Periodicals
060 General Organizations. Museums
070 Journalism, Newspapers
080 Special libraries
090 Rare Books

100-Philosophy and Psychology
110 Metaphysics
120 Knowledge, Purpose of man
130 Supernatural, Astrology, Dreams
140 Philosophical viewpoints
150 Psychology: Senses, Feelings, Friends
160 Logic
170 Ethics
180 Ancient, Oriental Philosophy
190 Modern, Western Philosophy

200-Religion
210 Natural Religion
220 Bible
230 Christianity
240 Christian Morals
250 Religious Orders
260 Theology, Church work
270 History of Religion
280 Christian denominations
290 Other Religions

300-Social Sciences
310 Statistics: People of the World
320 Political Science: Gov't, Civil Rights
330 Economics: Money, Energy
340 Law: Constitutional, Criminal, Social.
350 Presidents, Weapons, Military
360 Social Problems: Alcoholism, Disabilities
370 Education: Careers
380 Commerce, Transportation, Metric
390 Customs, Etiquette (398.2 Fairy tales)

400-Language
410 Speech and Language Books:
     Dictionaries
420 English
430 German
440 French
450 Italian
460 Spanish
470 Latin
480 Greek
490 Other: Rosetta Stone, Hieroglyphics

500-Natural Sciences / Mathematics
510 Mathematics
520 Astronomy: Space
530 Physics: Air, Magnets, Electricity
540 Chemistry: Water, Rocks/Gems
550 Geology: Weather, Earthquakes
560 Paleontology: Dinosaurs
570 Life Sciences: Biology, Ecosystems
580 Botany: Plants
590 Zoology: Animals, Insects, Fish, Birds

600-Technology
610 Medicine: Body, Drugs, Diseases
620 Engineering: Machines, Cars
630 Agriculture: Farm, Garden, Pets
640 Home Economics: Cook, Sew, Children
650 Management: Business, Secret Codes
660 Chemical Engineering: Gas and Oil
670 Manufacturing: Metals and Textiles
680 Make it Yourself: Instruments, Printing
690 Carpentry: Building things

700-The Arts
710 Landscape
720 Architecture
730 Sculpture
740 Drawing, Decorating, Design
750 Painting
760 Prints /Printmaking, Engraving
770 Photography
780 Music
790 Sports: Indoor & Outdoor

800-Literature and Poetry
810 American (811 Poetry, 812 Plays)
820 English (822 Shakespeare)
830 German
840 French
850 Italian
860 Spanish
870 Latin
880 Greek and Hellenic
890 Other

900-Geography and History
910 Geography, Countries of the World
920 Biography, Flag books
930 Ancient World: Egypt, Greece, Rome
940 History of Europe: World Wars I and II
950 History of Asia
960 History of Africa
970 History of North and Central America:
     Native Americans, State Books
980 History of South America
990 History of island nations

From *Practical Steps to the Research Process for High School* © 1999 Libraries Unlimited. 800-237-6124.

 **Instructor Information**

Balancing Instruction with Work Time

Lifelong Skills

The three days of lessons are over! Direct instruction in information management strategies must be equally balanced with hands-on library time for students to perform the research steps. Time to perform research tasks cannot be over-emphasized. The goal of these lectures is student independence in following the guide sheets and applying literacy and information literacy strategies to build lifelong skills for research success. Success is observable!

The first day of hands-on research, students come in eager to get started. That in itself is sometimes a change. Without this degree of preparation, have you noticed that, in the past, students approached research halfheartedly or not quite sure of what they were supposed to do, leaving them little choice but to copy information? Now, when I tell students that I have just a few instructions before they get started, I actually hear, "But I'm ready, I'm ready!"

Impatient to get started, students don't realize they have not received equipment access directions. These are the library skills which, in the past, have been mistaken for research instruction. Part of the paradigm shift for educational reform is putting the operation of hardware and software into its rightful place as tools to support the information literacy strategies of accessing, evaluating, and using information. Briefly, at the beginning of this fourth day, demonstrate to students some simple equipment procedures.

Information Literacy

Dewey/Boolean Handouts

To avoid dampening students' enthusiasm, give a brief explanation of *Figure 10-1*, Dewey Decimal System, for print materials and *Figure 10-2*, Boolean Logic, for the Internet. Regarding Dewey, it is my staggering experience when confronting high school students that many do not have card catalog access skills! Regarding the Internet, I do not expect students, or even teachers, to have a working knowledge of logical operators. The application of Boole's techniques is a start.

Technology Proficiency

Fig. 10-2. Boolean Logic

George Boole was a mathematician who devised a system of logical operators to retrieve information.

And

cars and red

Type the word *and* to tell your search tool that you want specific information. For example, typing only cars will give you all colors unless you specify: *cars and red.* Now you'll get only red cars.

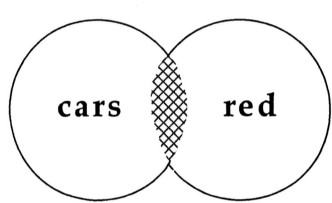

Or

cars or red

Type the word *or* to tell your search tool that you would be happy with either item. For example, you might be searching for pictures of all colors of cars *or* pictures of red cars, which means you'll be happy with pictures of both.

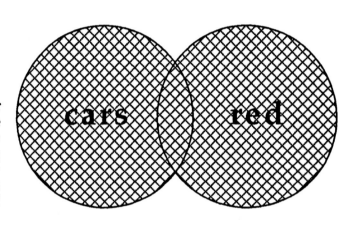

Not

cars not red

Type the word *not* to tell your search tool that you want to specifically exclude something. For example, typing *cars not red* will give you all colors of cars except red ones.

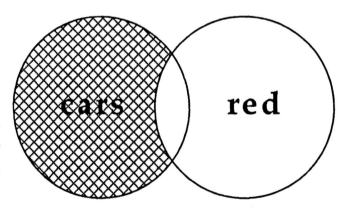

From *Practical Steps to the Research Process for High School* © 1999 Libraries Unlimited. 800-237-6124.

 **Student Lesson**

Print Sources: Using Dewey

Timing: 5 minutes.

LMT: This will only take a few minutes, I promise! I know you're anxious to get started today on your own research. Does anyone remember where you start first?

Student: An encyclopedia.

Student: The card catalog, on the computer.

LMT: You're both right. However, there are not enough computers for everyone to begin using the card catalog to look up books on your topic, so some of you head immediately back to the reference area. When you do get to the electronic card catalog and locate good sources, how do you find the book? (Blank stares!) Come on people, someone remembers! Look around you. What does every item have on it?

Student: A white tag on the back?

LMT: Which is called a "call tag." And it contains? Remember orientation in September when we located the nonfiction resources in this room, and I told you how to find them?

Student: Numbers.

LMT: Whew! Yes, that will be true for the nonfiction books for your history topics. Look at the Dewey sheet. Back in the 1800s, Melvil Dewey came up with a system to locate every kind of nonfiction book by assigning a number to its subject. On the sheet, do you see the 10 major subject classifications? It's obvious for your history project on World War II that you would probably not head off to the 200s because that's about religion. Or the 600s about technology. Right?

Let's see how well you can read and follow this guide sheet. If you wanted a computer book, where would you go?

Student: Zeros.

LMT: Good. A book on insects?

Student: The 500s.

LMT: More specifically?

Lifelong Skills

Content-Area Standard

**Content-Area
Standard**

**Important
Idea**

Student: The 590s.

LMT: World War II?

Student: 940s

LMT: Great. This is probably where you'll spend a lot of your time. I know you get it, but there's one other very important thing I'd like to call to your attention. Let's say you find a good book on the Holocaust in the 940s back in the nonfiction stacks. What happens when you go back to the reference area of the LMC? Do you have to look up "Holocaust" all over again? The good news is, it will also be there in the 940s! Make sense? How about if you went to the Oversize Books area?

Student: The 940s?

LMT: Absolutely. Videos?

Student: The 940s.

**Lifelong
Skills**

LMT: Perfect. This will help you for the rest of your life in every library that uses the Dewey system. Once you locate a source's call number, it will be the same in every format, or kind, of information. Works well, huh?

These Dewey guide sheets are always available here in the library. It's kind of like picking up a store directory in a huge home warehouse. You find what you want without wasting any time. Hasn't that been one of the main points in all of our research lessons? This sheet, (*Figure 10-1*), can get you to a specific area or shelf if you're in a hurry and all the card catalog stations are filled up. Walk around and match the sheet numbers with the aisle and shelf numbers. This is one of those handy-dandy things of life. You'll wonder how you ever lived without it.

Electronic Sources: Using Boolean

Timing: 5 minutes.

**Information
Literacy**

LMT: Now take a look at the Boolean Logic sheet (*Figure 10-2*). The Dewey System is for books; Boolean Logic is for computers. It's specifically helpful for a few of our computer search tools as well as the Internet. Full Internet orientation and instruction will be another day. Let me give just a few quick pointers for you to be aware of.

The top of your sheet says, "Boolean Logic." (LMT reads the top of the sheet about George Boole.) The technology term I want you to add to your vocabulary is, *logical operators*. Even some of you who are already designing your own web sites may not be using these tools effectively. I'll have handouts and special training for this another day, because it is very complex. Most of us think it's easy to use the Internet: Type your topic into a search engine and click on hot links. There's really a lot more to it than that.

The handout introduces you to three very basic Internet logical operators—*and*, *or*, and *not*—that can be used to tell the online search tool how to hunt for your topic more effectively. The sheet uses the example of cars, but let's think about a World War II topic such as the Holocaust. If you type in the simple keyword *Holocaust*, you'll get back absolutely every web site that particular search engine has access to, within the limitation of how many hits it displays at one time. But if you only want the effect of the Holocaust on children, type in *Holocaust and children*. It's confusing in the sense that you think you'd be getting both of those circles, but you're actually narrowing your search down to only very specific information about children who were involved in the Holocaust tragedy, nothing else. The word *and* is the most limiting of all the logical operators. Make sense?

Technology Proficiency

Let's look at the *or* circles. Let's say you want to know everything about the Holocaust *and* everything about children. You'd type in *Holocaust or children*.

Doesn't that seem opposite? Type "or" to get "and"?

When you type in two keywords connected by *or* you're really telling the Internet that you'd be happy with both! You'd be happy getting web sites all about the Holocaust or you'd be happy getting web sites all about children. You are getting both entire circles of information. So *or* is the most inclusive of the logical operators.

The last one is *not*. Let's say you wanted to learn about the Holocaust, but you don't have time to include anything in this report about children. You need to leave them out, so type in *Holocaust not children*. This is a little easier to understand. It's exactly as the circles on the sheet show you. If it's a Holocaust web site about children, it will be weeded out of the search.

Thanks for listening so patiently. Your teacher and I are both here to answer questions about anything that we've covered in the last few days, or anything about accessing information in any kind of source. You're a wonderful class. Let's get busy!

Chapter 11

Tracking and Evaluation

"The overall student output was much different this semester when we instructed the students on the research project."

—Collaborating teacher

Fig. 11-1. Adjusting the Research Process

Topic

- **Level of difficulty** of a topic is often determined by availability and readability of on-campus information.

- **Switching topics** is acceptable until the end of the first day of research. This increases interest while lowering frustration.

Subtopics

- **Simple is successful** for students' first experience with selecting subtopics.

- **Specific subtopics** that come directly from sources are great for young or lower functioning students. General subtopics often require higher thinking skills.

- **Switching subtopics** is fine any time during research. The criterion for switching is availability of information.

- **Number** of subtopics depends on teacher time and student ability. Remember, keep the project "do-able."

Sources

- **Use a combination** of print and electronic formats whenever possible. The number of sources is based on research time allowed.

- **Availability** of sources or of the library media center makes classroom "stations" a viable option. This makes excellent use of one or two classroom computers as well as limited books.

Read/Think/Select

- **Research reading strategies** require the teaching of skills and reinforcement with time for practice.

- **Automatic sequence** of reading, comprehension, evaluation, and selection of important information occurs during pencil-down quiet reading.

Notetake

- **One criterion** for a "good" note is the amount of writing generated. Good notetaking requires much practice.

- **Always collect** and quick-check notes. No reading is required of the teacher. Checking is the number one deterrent to plagiarism.

Sort and Number Notes

- **Whenever possible**, allow class time to begin sorting and numbering notes. This validates the notetaking effort.

From *Practical Steps to the Research Process for High School* © 1999 Libraries Unlimited. 800-237-6124.

Understanding Process vs. Project

Tracking students through research is based on the assumption that students have time to complete each of the research steps. Making time for each step is pacing. When teachers don't expose their students to directed research instruction, they may not understand pacing due to not understanding the Research Process. Do you know teachers who think they don't need research instruction? Perhaps they are confusing the parts of a research *project* with the steps of the *process*.

Once teachers become familiar with the Research Process, two things may happen. First, they realize that in the collaborative planning stage, each step of research can be adjusted (*Figure 11-1*) to meet their time frame or the special needs of their students. Second, when they clearly understand that research *has* steps, they tend to adopt more realistic project variables such as more time for research and less focus on quantity in favor of quality. The result is less student frustration and greater overall student success. Understanding that a research project syllabus does not address research strategies may awaken the need for information literacy collaborative instruction (*Figure 11-2*).

Fig. 11-2. Process vs. Project

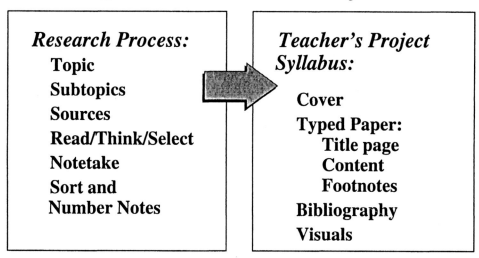

Research Process:
   Topic
   Subtopics
   Sources
   Read/Think/Select
   Notetake
   Sort and
   Number Notes

Teacher's Project Syllabus:

   Cover
   Typed Paper:
      Title page
      Content
      Footnotes
   Bibliography
   Visuals

From *Practical Steps to the Research Process for High School* © 1999 Libraries Unlimited. 800-237-6124.

Guidelines for Pacing Research

When the parts of a research project are confused with research strategies, pacing students through the project may be a guessing game for teachers. As a real example, a teacher assigned a tenth-grade class to write a 20-page research paper, due in two weeks, after the LMC had closed for year-end inventory! When I asked one of the students, "What is the class doing for information? Aren't they just copying as much as they can out of anything they can get their hands on?" He replied, "Oh, it doesn't matter She'll never read it anyway." Isn't the point of research to support standards and promote lifelong information literacy skills?

It wasn't just the unfortunate time of year which was unfair to the students with regard to information availability. On what basis does a teacher assign a 20-page paper? Research takes time. Based on past and current years of continuous collaborative research instruction, the following chart (Figure 11-3) provides practical benchmarks for pacing student research time on task. When time is an issue for teachers, the Research Process can offer a practical timetable of achievable steps which can therefore be paced and tracked (Figure 11-4). The result is both student accountability and greater success.

Fig. 11-3. Research Time on Task

Subtopics	Sources	Research Days	Notes	Pages
3	3	3	30	3
4	4	4	40	4
5	5	5	50	5
Special needs students: Reduce each level according to ability. **Advanced students:** The above criteria are a minimum.				

From *Practical Steps to the Research Process for High School* © 1999 Libraries Unlimited. 800-237-6124.

Student Tracking

Keeping tabs on student progress is not the isolated domain of the classroom teacher. During the initial collaborative planning, I always show the teacher an adapted form of the Research Tracking Sheet (*Figure 11-4*) and offer the following research support services:

- Offer to assist with tracking student progress at each step. Teachers will tell you right away if they don't want you involved. Some eagerly accept. For teachers whose research involvement is limited to the initial assignment and the final collection of a project, this is a novel idea! Your offer of time for tracking may be the single biggest factor in converting a teacher from focusing entirely on product to evaluating process. It is the evaluation of process that motivates students to accomplish information literacy tasks.

- Offer to type the class rosters into a template for each of the teacher's classes. This is a service that can be accomplished by dependable student assistants, and it reaps an enormous harvest of gratitude and converts to information literacy training.

- Adapt the tracking template to meet individual teacher needs. The computerized template can be easily altered by adjusting the number of columns and header titles to meet teacher time constraints, unit needs, and special student requirements.

- Adjust the coding of student progress to match each teacher's style and needs. Some teachers want a quick minus sign, check mark, or plus sign to mark progress. Some teachers like the 0–3 number code at the bottom of the sheet. I have always recorded exact amounts accomplished for each step. For example, a 5, 8, or 3 in the "Sources" column reflects exactly how many sources the student used. Thirty-two, 17, or 28 shows exactly how many notes were accomplished compared to the day's goal. This sounds like a lot of work, but it's not! I guarantee this is easily accomplished in the last few minutes of class, especially if you divide the tracking with the teacher. "Have your notes counted," the LMT announces. Then you can walk quickly among the students without even disturbing them. The effect on students of this daily tracking to produce a better quality product with a higher rate of both learning and creativity cannot be overstated. This simply works!

Information Literacy

Content-Area Standard

ELL/Special Modifications

Fig. 11-4. Research Tracking Sheet

Teacher: ‗‗‗‗‗‗‗ Period: ‗‗‗‗‗‗‗ **Student Names**	Topic Subtopics	Sources	10 Notes	10 Notes	10 Notes	10 Notes	10 Notes	Rough Draft	Bibliography	Enrichment	Final Project	**TOTAL**

Scoring: 3 = Independent   2 = Needs assistance   1 = Deficient   0 or (ab)

From *Practical Steps to the Research Process for High School* © 1999 Libraries Unlimited. 800-237-6124.

Library Media Program Accountability

The self-evidence of the value of the library media program to promote literacy and information literacy through collaboration in standards-based units of study does not exempt it from site and district accountability. Like every other field with a genuine curriculum, accountability validates its successes and points to areas of improvement.

Experience in the field suggests that the form of evaluation should match the program. In this case, the Research Process is only taught through the curriculum of other subject areas. The advantage is its relevance to real-life tasks. The greatest disadvantage may be the impact of time on already over-extended teachers. Therefore, upon completion of a unit with a collaborative partner, avoid asking teachers to fill out evaluation paperwork. If that isn't possible, keep the form simple, like *Figure 11-5*.

It may be advantageous for the LMT to debrief with teachers informally with the same, "I'll catch you at lunch," manner used in the initial unit planning. With or without a simple evaluation template, make mental notes about what worked and what didn't! As in the original planning sheet, the LMT can later update the computer template and put an amended copy of that unit into the teacher's mailbox. The teacher will love it, and so will the LMT! Besides making specific unit alterations, record anecdotal comments. In this way, over time the LMT builds a critical evaluation database to document future projects such as grants or administrative reports. Of more practical value is a finely tuned unit for that content area. Eventually, the result is a huge, readily retrievable database of lessons and units for all grade levels at the site.

On a more formal level it is difficult, if not impossible, to come up with a standardized testing procedure for the library media program. For those administrators or board members who demand statistics to validate the hiring of library media teachers, the improvement over time in school-wide test scores must logically be a hoped-for effect.

The subjective results of a successful library media program may be seen every single day in the increase in a school-wide model for collaborative instruction, the point of which would be grass-roots support of this program and not of any particular personality. If it is generally true that, "People make the program," then for library media, "The program empowers the people who teach it and the people who are taught." This program is absolutely essential to educational reform.

Fig. 11-5. Unit Evaluation Sheet

Teacher: _____ Grade: _____ Period: _____

Unit: _____ Date: _____

What worked well:

What didn't work:

From *Practical Steps to the Research Process for High School* © 1999 Libraries Unlimited. 800-237-6124.

Chapter 12

Writing the Rough Draft

"Boundaries empower creativity."
　　　　　　　　—Deborah Stanley

"I can't believe what this student has written! Before, she was hardly able to write a few sentences."
　　　　　　　—Language arts teacher

Fig. 12-1. Empower Composing

For the Student

Voice: The writer
- The imprint of ourselves on our writing.
- An engaging voice will hold the reader's interest.

Audience: The reader
- To whom is the writing directed?
- The intended reader determines the tone of the writing.

Sharing: Critiquing
- Sharing aloud separates the *content* from the *mechanics*, so students distinguish revising writing from editing errors.
- Criticism guidelines: A suggestion for improvement should be preceded by a positive observation.
- Hearing and responding to each other's work is the single most powerful tool to empower students' composing.

Reading: Literate Learning
- Read to Write! Immersion in reading will build vocabulary, concepts, and interest in writing.
- Read outside sources: a variety of genres, fiction, and nonfiction, to increase knowledge for writing.
- Read student work: Re-read your own and other students' rough drafts to revise and edit for self-improvement and for peer validation.

For the Instructor

Teacher: The empowering agent
- Question constructively to empower writing.
- Establish boundaries and strategies for student questions.
- Topic, content, and intent can be good sources of questions.

Environment: The empowering situation
- A risk-free environment comes from constant sharing and encouragement to promote fluency and creativity in writing.

From *Practical Steps to the Research Process for High School* © 1999 Libraries Unlimited. 800-237-6124.

Making Time

What is the most effective way to validate the entire Research Process? A simple question addresses the urgent need to encourage good writing and prevent plagiarism:

Do you make time for student writing?

Important Idea

Whether you teach science, history, math, or English, scheduling one period to kick off writing the rough draft validates all steps of the Research Process and empowers students to write from notes. With the teacher as facilitator, all of the Empower Composing elements (*Figure 12-1*) can take place. Without scheduled time, perhaps none of it will occur, and yet the expectation of an excellent product remains.

Education is in the midst of a literacy crisis, and the only way for students to learn to read and to improve reading is to engage in reading. Writing is very much a part of literacy, and the same situation occurs. The only way to learn to write and to improve writing is to write. Following the instruction of research strategies, both of these needs are met by allocating time. When the teacher/facilitator schedules time to begin the rough draft, more than writing occurs. The ingredients of validated notes, teacher questioning, time to write, and student sharing and feedback magically combine into creative empowerment. I believe this is putting our "money where our mouth is" for educational reform.

Literacy

Process Writing

Teachers may not make time for writing for the same reason they don't teach practical research steps: They may be unfamiliar with strategies for promoting good writing. A well known, comprehensive source of sequential writing strategies is a course in process writing. As a classroom teacher, I had the fortunate experience of attending a branch of the Bay Area Writing Project. This was a seminal, life-changing event for me. My whole approach, not only to the teaching of writing but to teaching in general, was forever changed.

I count my classroom experience with process writing as one of the critical areas of training which made me a better library media teacher. So much so that whenever possible, I advocate this being added as a preservice class for library media teacher credentialing. Because I knew *where* I was heading with good research, I had a much better idea of *what* I needed to do to bring students to that point.

Prior to teaching high school, I had library media teacher experiences in elementary and then in middle school, where my collaborative teaching partners were delighted to make time for me to kick off composing the rough draft following the completion of notetaking. High school teachers were especially astonished that an LMT would do this, but if time permits, isn't this a logical extension? There are strategies for students' successful use of notes which validate the entire Research Process.

In reality, a quick view of the steps of process writing (*Figure 12-2*) shows that the only writing stages available to the library media teacher would be the prewriting step and briefly, the composing step. Beg for that!

Fig. 12-2. Process Writing

Prewriting
Notetaking/Motivational lessons and reading

Composing
Information + Creativity + Time = Fluency

Revising
Changing the content

Editing
Correcting the mechanics

Publishing
Audience other than the writer

From *Practical Steps to the Research Process for High School* © 1999 Libraries Unlimited. 800-237-6124.

Getting Started

If the teacher allows the LMT a period to begin writing the rough draft with students, hopefully it is preceded by a period of direct instruction for sorting, sequencing, and numbering notes. Once students understand these strategies, what isn't finished in class is easily completed as homework. What's important is that they arrive on writing day with notes entirely processed and numbered. Remind them to bring a couple of sheets of notebook paper to class. Arrange *not* to share the LMC with another class that day because writing requires quiet thought. With these things in place, students are physically ready to write, but are they mentally ready?

Writing the Introduction

"Is your first note the first sentence in your research paper?" Depending on the content area, the answer is, "No." With this question, I kick off these valuable moments of helping students convert their hard-earned research into a rough draft. Students often respond to this question with blank stares. Without instruction, the usual student reaction to *every* step of research is this exact same confusion. This alone is validation for collaborative teaching of Research Process strategies!

Students have their Research Checklist (*Figure 8-8*) in front of them which lists their topic and subtopics. This guide sheet is where the first paragraph comes from, so their pile of note pages or cards should be turned upside down. (You should see the looks that instruction gets!) "Does anyone know how your paper should begin?" I ask. What I am leading students up to is the need for an introduction. "You need to tell the reader what your paper is going to be about. It's like reading the summary on the back of a novel to decide whether to read the book." For the sake of time, give specific instructions for creating an introductory paragraph:

Step 1: The first sentence or two of a research paper should state the topic and define it for the reader.

Step 2: Each of the subtopics becomes a separate sentence telling what will be covered in each section of the paper. In other words, students should write at least one entire introductory paragraph before they begin writing from their notes. I find this guided exercise, with much sharing aloud, very helpful in getting students to set writing goals. They then write with greater confidence!

Prewriting

Prewriting is the mental motivation to compose. Because writing time with students is so limited, the primary motivation is, of course, their notes combined with both prior and new knowledge from their research. It is also extremely beneficial to read samples of previous students' papers. Here are a few simple steps to proceed with prewriting:

Literacy

Step 1: Allow a minimum of five uninterrupted minutes for students to begin reading notes they have designated as subtopic, or section, one. They should read the notes in number order. The only sound permitted at this time is paper shuffling as they locate notes. Call "time" no matter how far students have gotten.

Step 2: Have students use the person next to them as a partner. Allow five minutes for the first person to begin "telling" their paper to the partner, composing aloud from sequential notes. Allow another five minutes for students to reverse roles. "If you can say it, you can write it," says the LMT.

Composing

ELL/Special Modifications

Students are now ready to begin writing from their notes to create the body of the paper. Dividing a project into sections, subtopic by subtopic, may seem like a very simplistic way to tackle writing, especially at the high school level. Unfortunately, given the language and ability levels of many students, they seem to need all the guidance they can get. I firmly believe that creativity springs from structure, not from a vacuum. For this reason, I make available the Descriptive Word lists (*Figures 12-3* and *12-4*) to remind them to make research writing more interesting with accurate adjectives. They should select parts of speech which support the original information.

Important Idea

For the remainder of the period, alternate 10 to 15 minutes of quiet writing with a few minutes of sharing time. This is the most important thing that could happen in the entire period. Call for volunteers who would like to read their introductions to the class. Model clapping when each reader has finished, and students will join in. Make a positive comment about the way something was done, and ask what someone else may have noticed that was working well. You immediately see the positive effects of this sharing time. Some students appreciate validation of their own work, others absorb ideas for improvement. The point is, they absolutely learn best from each other. When the bell rings, students have a great start on an original piece of work! The LMT's work is done.

Fig. 12-3. Descriptive Word List, A–I

absurd	clever	disgraced	fictitious
abundant	clobbered	disobedient	fierce
abusive	clumped	disputed	fidgety
accurate	comical	dreary	flamboyant
adventurous	comfortable	dreadful	flawless
affectionate	commendable	dreamy	flexible
aggressive	commotion	dramatic	flimsy
agitated	compassionate	dribbled	foolish
aimless	complex	dumbfounded	forceful
ambitious	competitive	earnest	foreign
ample	conceited	eager	forgiving
ancient	complicated	eccentric	fragile
animated	confused	ecstatic	freaky
annoyed	consistent	effective	fortunate
appealing	conservative	eerie	frail
artificial	considerate	elaborate	frenzied
attractive	continuous	elated	frustrated
austere	crushed	embarrassed	frightened
awkward	courageous	emerged	frumpy
babbling	critical	emotional	gallant
barbaric	curious	encountered	gentle
beastly	dainty	endless	genuine
beautiful	dashing	encourage	ghastly
befuddled	dawdled	energetic	gleaming
believable	dangerous	enduring	gloomy
belligerent	dazed	enjoyable	glorious
beneficial	debatable	entangled	griped
benevolent	decent	enormous	growled
biased	dedicated	enthusiastic	gulped
bickering	defective	envious	hasty
blazing	deliberate	essential	harsh
blotched	delicate	especially	heroic
bloodthirsty	delirious	exaggerated	hesitated
blubbered	delightful	excessive	hopeless
blundered	dependable	exhausted	horrible
busybody	deplorable	exquisite	howled
calm	depressed	extravagant	hotheaded
capable	descriptive	fabulous	humorous
cantankerous	destroyed	faded	hypocrite
candid	destitute	familiar	ideal
charming	determined	fantastic	ignorant
cheerful	detected	fascinating	illustrated
chilly	devoted	fateful	imaginative
childish	disastrous	feeble	immense
clashing	discouraged	filthy	imbecile

From *Practical Steps to the Research Process for High School* © 1999 Libraries Unlimited. 800-237-6124.

Fig. 12-4. Descriptive Word List, I–Z

immortal	lenient	neglectful	perceived
impatient	lighthearted	nimble	pessimistic
imply	liberated	noble	persuaded
mposing	lively	nonsense	pitiful
impressive	logical	notable	pleasant
impressionable	lonesome	noticeable	pondered
improper	lopsided	nuisance	positively
impulsive	lovely	nutritious	precious
inappropriate	luxurious	obedient	presumably
inarticulate	magical	obese	profound
incredible	magnificent	objectionable	provocative
incompatible	malicious	obligated	punctual
inconsolable	manipulated	obnoxious	quarrelsome
indecisive	manufactured	obscene	quiet
indifferent	marvelous	obscure	radical
indignant	mature	observed	random
indulge	meaningless	obsolete	reasonable
inevitable	melodious	obstacle	recognizable
inexcusable	memorialize	occasionally	refreshing
inferior	merchandise	occupied	reliable
infallible	merciful	offensive	relevant
informal	meticulous	officially	remarkable
ingenious	meddling	ominous	respectful
inflammatory	migrated	opinionated	restless
inflexible	mingled	opportunity	reckless
innovative	miniature	oppressive	rowdy
initiative	mischievous	opponent	sarcastic
inquiring	miserable	optimistic	satisfying
insincere	misfortune	optional	scholarly
insensitive	misunderstanding	organized	scenic
insignificant	mistaken	ornate	scavenge
insufficient	mocked	outrageous	secluded
insulting	moaned	outspoken	sensitive
intelligent	modern	outwitted	serious
intimidating	monotonous	overacted	shocking
investigate	modest	overlapped	successful
irritating	morbid	oversight	tedious
irrational	motivated	overwhelm	terrifying
jealous	mournful	painful	truthful
jittery	muffled	panted	uncontrollable
justified	multitude	paraded	vulgar
kooky	mumbled	pardoned	vulnerable
knowledgeable	mysterious	participant	wallow
laborious	narrow	particular	wisdom
lavish	nasty	passionate	yield
legitimate	nauseating	patriotic	zoom

From *Practical Steps to the Research Process for High School* © 1999 Libraries Unlimited. 800-237-6124.

Section 4

Enrichment and
Extension

Chapter 13
The Creative Final Project

Chapter 14
Technology Supports Research

Chapter 15
Connections

185

Chapter 13

The Creative Final Project

"The reality of life is that we are judged by appearances. Fortunately, teachers also have content rubrics."

—History Day, Judge

Fig. 13-1. Creative Presentation Ideas

Writing	Projects	Presentations	Technology

Advertisement:
• Brochure
• Newspaper
• Oral
Book-making
Chart
Crossword puzzle
Diary:
• Log
• Journal
Editorial
Epitaph
Graph
Index
Letter
Newspaper story
Music lyrics
Poetry:
• Couplets
• Cinquains
• Diamante
• Haiku
• Limericks
Proverb
Quiz
Resumé
Review
Writing domains:
• Story
• Report of
  Information
• Evaluation
• Description
• Persuasion
• Narration
• Essay
	Banner
	Bulletin Board
	Bumper sticker
	Cartoon
	Collage
	Diorama
	Display
	Drawing
	Flannel board
	Game
	License plate
	  slogan
	Map
	Mobile
	Model
	Mural
	Photography
	Poster
		Banquet
		Cassette tape
		  recording
		Commentary
		Debate
		Demonstration
		Dialogue
		Drama / Play
		Experiment
		Fair
		Interview
		Lecture
		Lesson
		Mime
		Mock trial
		Panel discussion
		Pantomime
		Puppetry
		Radio program
		Role playing
		Round Table
		Simulation
		Skit
		TV program
			CD-ROM image
			Chat room, ie.:
			  with authors
			Claris slide show
			Computer art
			Desktop publishing
			Digital camera
			  images
			E-mail pen pals
			HyperStudio stack
			Internet images
			Laser disk clips
			  and frames
			Multimedia
			  presentation
			Overhead
			  transparency
			PowerPoint
			  presentation
			QuickCam clips
			  or frames
			Scanner images
			T-shirts
			Video production
			Web page
			  construction

From *Practical Steps to the Research Process for High School* © 1999 Libraries Unlimited. 800-237-6124.

Beyond Writing

The Research Process focuses on, as the name implies, the *process* it takes to produce a research product. However, do you find that your educational situation is still mostly product oriented? The accountability factor is ever present. Therefore, it is important to have a chapter which addresses the issue of final products to validate the usefulness and practical application of the Research Process.

Discussion of a final product naturally seems to fall at the conclusion of research. In reality, the Creative Presentation Ideas sheet seen in *Figure 13-1* is absolutely the *first* thing teachers need to consider at the beginning of collaborative planning! This is the first question that should be asked:

> *What do you want to accomplish with this research project?*

Will the project supplement and enrich the content-area unit in progress, teach research skills and information management, address a specific technology need, cover a writing domain, or provide an attractive display of student work for Open House? The idea sheet helps shift the educational paradigm to more interesting, student-centered activities.

Content-Area Standard

Are many of the teachers at your high school still requiring a written paper as the product, or is your school establishing educational reforms which mean more hands-on lessons and creative efforts? I believe it is inherent in the library media program to aim toward creative innovations in the final product as the corollary to the information literacy focus on process.

Information Literacy

Seeing the excitement as a teacher realizes the possibilities of a radio talk show script, a banner, or a laser disk video clip incorporated into an oral report makes being a library media teacher one of the most innovative jobs in education. The synergy from the initial collaborative planning creates an extra energy that spills over into the research lessons. Students, in turn, get excited about what they will be producing, and information acquisition takes on a whole new meaning.

Important Idea

Fig. 13-2. Technology-Enriched Report

Rwanda Fact Box

Population: 8,000,000 people (est.-1996)
Land area: 10,169,000 sq. mi.
Natural Resources: tin, wolframite
Manufacturing: agriculture, coffee
Capital City: Kigali

Image inserted from:

Digital Camera
Internet
CD-ROM
Software clip art library
Scanner

Rwanda
Mr. Doe, Periods 5/6, January 1997

In this report you will learn about a country in Africa by the name
of Rwanda. First, you will learn about the people as they lived in
history and as they live now. Then, you will understand some other
events that took place in the history of this interesting country. Next,
you will experience what the land and climate of Rwanda is like.
Finally, you will learn about their economics and what makes them

From *Practical Steps to the Research Process for High School* © 1999 Libraries Unlimited. 800-237-6124.

Exciting Writing!

If writing a report is the desired choice for presenting information, it is important that students know how to extend a written report into a rich, visually instructional experience. The insertion of images into all parts of a report (*Figure 13-2*) from title page, to main body, to addendum, creates a more interesting, appealing, and informative project. (Be *sure* to cover copyright and Fair Use laws.) Here are some of the ways in which images can be retrieved and inserted into word processed or desktop published student reports:

Technology Proficiency

CD-ROM: A huge variety of CD-ROMs are currently available which contain nothing but images. Copyright is not a problem because the purpose of such CD-ROMs is the unlimited use of the images they contain. Simply cut and paste!

Computer software: As with CD-ROMs, computer software is available for images. Some are for the express purpose of providing images for unlimited use. Draw programs enable students to create hand-drawn images for insertion into reports. While exciting for all students, this feature is especially interesting and educationally rewarding to special needs students. An example of a drawing created by an ELL (English Language Learner) student learning about America appears in *Figure 13-3*.

ELL/Special Modifications

Laser disks: The advantage here is the ability to insert either still frames or video clips into multimedia presentation programs. Cost does not have to be a factor because many district and county central libraries house marvelous laser disk collections begging to be borrowed.

Scanner: From the small, black and white, hand-held scanner to a color flatbed scanner, all prices and quality ranges of scanners are available. This is perhaps the easiest, most accessible way for students to insert images found in books into their reports. Again, teach students about copyright and Fair Use.

Internet: Have you recently typed *free clip art* into an Internet search engine? You will come up with a mind boggling panorama of choices. Because it is incredibly easy to copy and paste Internet images, copyright privileges are often clearly explained on web sites. Fair Use may apply for student reports.

Fig. 13-3. Hand-Drawn Computer Map Inserted in Report

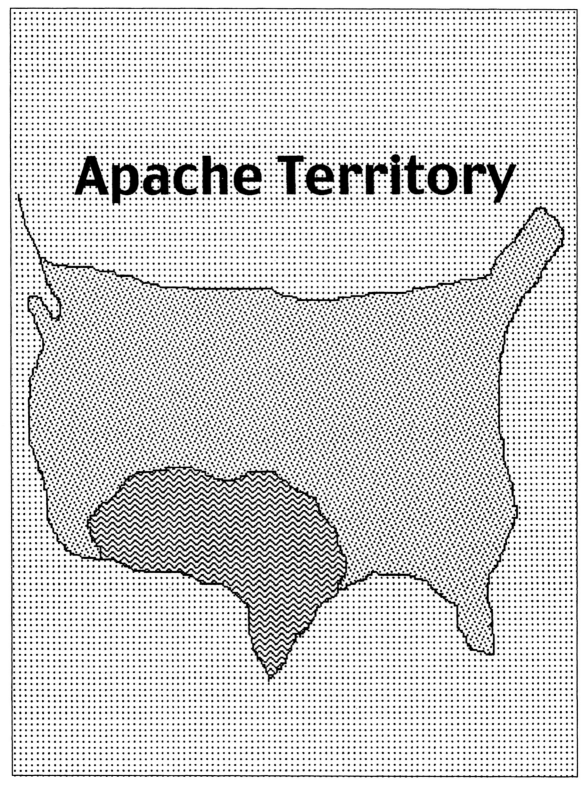

From *Practical Steps to the Research Process for High School* © 1999 Libraries Unlimited. 800-237-6124.

The Power of the Laser Disk

The students who participated in the image insertion project in *Figure 13-2* commented that creating the report was the best time they "ever had!" Their teachers included many of the reports in student portfolios because, as was said by more than one teacher,

"This is the first thing that student has completed all year! They are all so proud of their work."

But let's set aside the obvious ways to create visually appealing reports and focus on a way to create magnificently high-interest reports. Have you used a laser disk lately? It was often the case that by the time the school finally got around to buying a laser disk player, it was shoved into the corner as the stampede to go "on-line" gathered momentum. With the increase in DVD technology, laser disks basically died out, except in science classrooms, before they ever caught on.

"What good is an old laser disk player anyway?" Amazingly good! There must be one sitting in a storeroom, or in a corner of the library media center, that no one seems to know what to do with. Latch onto it! As previously noted, you can probably get hold of highly unit-specific disks in your district, site, or county central library, *free*! Tell teachers you'll coordinate their content-area curriculum with district and county media catalogs. Then, borrow a laser disk that a teacher would love, and invite them to the LMC for a preview. Once a teacher sits down with the remote control and the manual of image numbers or barcodes and starts scanning, a whole new world opens up! Unlike videos, with a laser disk they quickly discover how easy it is to navigate to still frames or video segments that exactly fit both the point of the lesson and the usually limited teaching time frame.

"Wow! Who's been hiding this?" *you'll soon hear.*

The next discovery for the teacher is how laser disks can spice up student reports. Follow the directions in *Figure 13-4* to have students create barcodes, paste them onto their reports at strategic spots, and wand with the barcode reader during their oral presentations. This works!

Technology Proficiency

Fig. 13-4. Creating Laser Disk Barcodes

Set up the following:

1. Open *Enhanced Bar 'n Coder*.
2. Click on NO PLAYER.
3. Click on W/PROMPTS.
4. Click on:
   PLAY FRAMES (for a clip)
   FRAME SEARCH (for a still frame)
5. Click on MAKE CODE at bottom.
6. Type in barcode number.

Follow all on-screen prompts:

7. Check "Settings" at left / DONE.
8. Bar code now appears.
9. "Want descriptive labels?" / YES.
10. "Type label caption" / DONE.
11. "Print frame numbers?" / YES.
12. "Transfer code to..." / PAPER PAGE.
13. "Ready for transfer to printing?" / YES

Conclude procedure:

14. Barcode page appears.
15. To print: in lower right, click on: "Print this card."
16. To start over: In lower left, click on: "Return to Bar 'n Coder."

From *Practical Steps to the Research Process for High School* © 1999 Libraries Unlimited. 800-237-6124.

Chapter 14

Technology Supports Research

*"I've never seen a labor-saving device
which requires so much time and labor!"*
—Technology teacher
(referring to computers)

Fig. 14-1. Supporting Research in Many Ways

 Library Media Teacher

COLLABORATIVE TEACHER	The library media teacher: • Collaboratively plans lessons to teach and evaluate students to access, evaluate, and use information. • Integrates the information literacy curriculum into the standards-based curriculum of the school and district. • Integrates technology as a tool of information management through on-site resources and off-site networking. • Models excellent teaching strategies and uses a variety of instructional methods with different user groups.
INFORMATION SPECIALIST	• Evaluates and selects resources for purchase through a careful review process. Makes resources available to teachers and students through a systematically developed collection within the school and access to information outside the site. • Weeds out resources which contain inaccurate information as a result of age, stereotypes, and new developments. • Continually learns about new technologies, trains in their use, reviews for applicability to school site information needs, and seeks funding if acquisition is feasible. • Arranges class visits flexibly to encourage point of need and equitable access to all formats of information and to the library media center qualified staff. • Advocates and instructs students, teachers, and community members about the laws and policies regarding the legal use of information (copyright).
INSTRUCTIONAL PARTNER	• Regularly participates in district and site curriculum development and assessment projects. • Assists teachers in assessing instructional materials and incorporating information literacy skills into the classroom curriculum. • Assists administration and staff in planning, selecting, and implementing new technologies throughout the site.
PROGRAM ADMINISTRATOR	• Interprets the goals and objectives of information literacy for students, teachers, and the community. Applies these goals and objectives through a collaborative instructional program. • Establishes a vision calling for every individual to be information literate. Knowledgeably carries forward this mission by linking school needs to the world of information. • Is proficient and efficient in facility management including budget, personnel, technology, and positive environment.

From *Practical Steps to the Research Process for High School* © 1999 Libraries Unlimited. 800-237-6124.

Technology: The LMT's Toolbox

Technology Proficiency

On every campus there are teachers who are technology wizards. Is the library media teacher included in that number? This chapter will offer examples of technology integration into almost every facet of the LMT's job description (*Figure 14-1*), especially the teaching of the Research Process, making inclusion in the campus "tech nerds" group almost a foregone conclusion.

But what good are technology tools if you are unsure of your role? LMTs may suffer from an identity crisis, particularly when they first enter the field. In the beginning, not knowing the extent of the job is a blessing in disguise by preventing the LMT from being overwhelmed by the enormity of the position. However, as change agents, innovators, and trend setters, library media teachers must dynamically and proactively embrace fast growth.

Information Power identifies four basic roles of the library media teacher: collaborative teacher, information specialist, instructional consultant, and program manager. Personal role definition within the campus and district becomes the obvious first task to which an LMT can apply technology. *Figure 14-1* is a job description to give as a handout to teacher groups and administrators. The technology used in creating this form assumes a working knowledge of any integrated suite of applications which includes a word processing program containing draw, spreadsheet, and clip art functions. What better kickoff to introduce the paradigm shift the LMT wishes to promote than to creatively advertise yourself in order to define the role in terms of "change agent" responsibilities.

You are your own best billboard.

This chapter will offer a technology toolbox of hardware and software examples, according to the four globally understood roles, to enable LMTs to better match technology tools to the Research Process. The obvious disclaimer is the rendering of these samples obsolete due to the almost unimaginable rapidity of technology evolution. Therefore, hardware and software will be identified generically, with a suggestion attached to each example for the LMT to be acquainted with, for example, a color scanner or a desktop publishing application.

The LMT's Role As Collaborative Teacher

One of the reasons new library media teachers are recruited from the ranks of experienced classroom teachers is that they are expected to enter the field not only with teaching experience, but as exemplary educators with excellent knowledge of curriculum, instruction, classroom management, and discipline strategies. From the first day, LMTs must command the respect of their peers as role models of collaborative teaching.

What makes other teachers *want* to begin collaborating with the LMT for research instruction? Someone once said that trying to get teachers to move in a new educational direction is like herding cats. We all have different ideas. Teachers face the curious dichotomy of being expected by their students to "know everything" and being expected by administration to learn new teaching standards and strategies. Sometimes, collaborating with an LMT is beyond the comfort zone for teachers who feel they do not need assistance in their content area. Other times, teachers are happy to ask the LMT to show a class how to use a piece of equipment or a new program, but that is *not* collaborative teaching! The answer, of course, is for each LMT to develop his or her own strategies for the Research Process and to model research instruction which integrates technology.

Content-Area Standard

Figure 14-2. The Teacher's Planning Calendar kicks off the new school year with a template for the planning of instructional units integrated with technology. Using this, teachers can coordinate units with other department members to alternate use of the library media center and the services of the LMT for research instruction. Benefits include greater collaboration and sharing of innovative ideas and teaching strategies among department members who often have little time to spare for meeting with colleagues. Converting teachers to global planning also promotes the conscientious covering of standards-based units necessary for student accountability.

Technology Proficiency

Figure 14-3. The Student Technology Challenge models a major role of the library media teacher which is to provide instruction and assistance in the use of technology to access and use information directly integrated into content-area units of study. Can the students perform all of these basic technology functions? This chart is a condensation of district and state technology proficiencies adapted to information literacy expectations.

Fig. 14-2. Teacher's Planning Calendar

(Subject)		

September	Unit:	**February**	Unit:
1 2 3 4 5		2 3 4 5 6	
8 9 10 11 12	Project:	9 10 11 12 13	Project:
15 16 17 18 19		16 17 18 19 20	
22 23 24 25 26		23 24 25 26 27	
29 30	Technology:		Technology:

October	Unit:	**March**	Unit:
1 2 3		2 3 4 5 6	
6 7 8 9 10	Project:	9 10 11 12 13	Project:
13 14 15 16 17		16 17 18 19 20	
20 21 22 23 24		23 24 25 26 27	
27 28 29 30 31	Technology:	30 31	Technology:

November	Unit:	**April**	Unit:
3 4 5 6 7		1 2 3	
10 11 12 13 14	Project:	6 7 8 9 10	Project:
17 18 19 20 21		13 14 15 16 17	
24 25 26 27 28		20 21 22 23 24	
	Technology:	27 28 29 30	Technology:

December	Unit:	**May**	Unit:
1 2 3 4 5		1	
8 9 10 11 12	Project:	4 5 6 7 8	Project:
15 16 17 18 19		11 12 13 14 15	
22 23 24 25 26		18 19 20 21 22	
29 30 31	Technology:	25 26 27 28 29	Technology:

January	Unit:	**June**	Unit:
1 2		1 2 3 4 5	
5 6 7 8 9	Project:	8 9 10 11 12	Project:
12 13 14 15 16		15 16 17 18 19	
19 20 21 22 23			
26 27 28 29 30	Technology:		Technology:

From *Practical Steps to the Research Process for High School* © 1999 Libraries Unlimited. 800-237-6124.

Fig. 14-3. Student Technology Challenge

Demonstrate all your technology skills. Choose a simple topic to create a report and a presentation using each of the following activities.

Access information:

- Access print resources using an electronic card catalog.
- Access information in a CD-ROM electronic encyclopedia.
- Access Internet information (web site/online search tool).
- Use an online interactive web site to converse/consult with a person or institution about your topic.

Evaluate information:

- Use a spreadsheet or database to interpret or demonstrate report information.
- Plot information with a graph program. (It could be a timeline.)

Use information:

- Use a word processor to type your report.
- Enhance your oral report with a laser disk frame or clip via a barcode you created and pasted into the script.
- Use a draw program to create a map or diagram about some aspect of your report.
- Insert images into your report (be aware of copyright restrictions):
    - Take a digital camera picture and insert it on the title page.
    - Copy and paste an Internet image into the body of the report.
    - Locate an image in a book. Copy it on the color scanner. Save it to a disk or electronically transfer it to your report.
- Create a multimedia presentation about your topic incorporating an audio clip and a still frame or movie clip from a laser disk, a digital camera, or a video camera.

Enrichment challenge:

- Collaborate with a friend or a group and create an Internet web site about your topic.

From *Practical Steps to the Research Process for High School* © 1999 Libraries Unlimited. 800-237-6124.

The LMT's Role As Information Specialist

In the role of information specialist, the library media teacher is a site mentor for print and nonprint resources available on campus balanced against awareness of innovative, new resources. Acquisitions should be balanced against timely weeding of the collection. The LMT's astute ability to match appropriate sources of information with curricular units of study in all content areas and at all grade levels is a prerequisite to effective collaborative teaching.

An extension of this capacity is the vital role of guardian and instructor of copyright and information use policies. The most current information on copyright for print and nonprint resources as well as "netiquette," appropriate use of networked information, is available by simply typing *copyright* or *netiquette* into any search engine on the Internet. The information specialist role may also include:

Figure 14-4. Tiger Tracks: LMC Orientation can help the LMT kick off a new school year with a hands-on activity to introduce new students to information location in all print and nonprint LMC resources.

Figure 14-5. Search Tips helps out when there are more services to provide than the LMT can possibly have time for! Does basic management of the LMC facility preclude time for training students to access all of the print and nonprint resources which is basic to information management? Then self-directed stations set up with student direction sheets are a life-saving solution. For example, one way for an LMT to be "everywhere at once" is to write direction sheets for specific points of information access. This all-in-one Search Tips sheet hangs on the side of every computer in the library media center so that it is readily available to students even after beginning-of-the-year orientation. Books and equipment shouldn't gather dust because an individual can't physically stand there and give directions for use.

Figure 14-6. The Internet: Graphically Speaking shows that less is more! The Internet, which appears so simple for high school students to use, is actually a highly complex and ever-changing phenomenon. This orientation sheet attempts to convey global concepts combined with a practical understanding of Internet searching for those time-stressed teachers who still want a meaningful orientation for students new to the school or to the Internet.

Fig. 14-4. Tiger Tracks: LMC Orientation

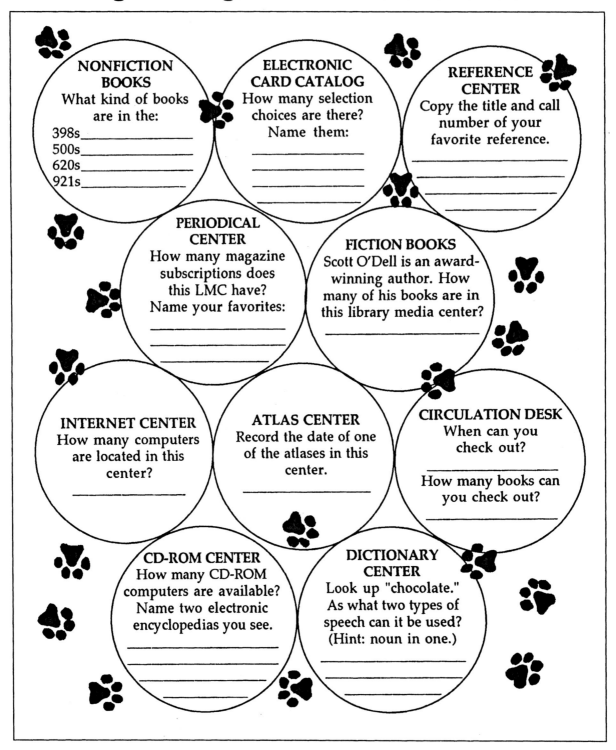

From *Practical Steps to the Research Process for High School* © 1999 Libraries Unlimited. 800-237-6124.

Fig. 14-5. Search Tips

PRINT RESOURCES: Begin your search with the Computer Card Catalog.

Fiction/nonfiction books ....**Double click** *Card Catalog* icon / Wait.
Type subject*, title, or author / ENTER.
   (* Remember to type a person's last name first.)
Follow bottom menu commands to navigate.
Copy call # on left. Match with shelf labels.

Biography...**Use** Current Biography Yearbooks (green volumes).

Encyclopedias...**Use** Index (usually the last volume in a set).
Look up topic in alphabetical order by volume.

Periodicals (magazines)..............................**Current issues** are in alphabetical order in racks.
Back issues are best located electronically.

Newspapers.. ....**Today's papers** are labeled on newspaper rack.
Back issues are accessed in computers, online.

NONPRINT: Electronic information from computers.

World Book Multimedia Encyclopedia. ....**Double click** icon / See hourglass / Wait.
Click SEARCH on Main Menu.
Type your topic (last name first for a person).
Use outline on left for quick access to text.
Use SEARCH icon to navigate to another topic
Quit when done by using X in upper right.

Encarta Encyclopedia '97..........................**Double click** icon / See hourglass / Wait.
Click *encyclopedia articles* for most searches.
Type topic in type-bar in left menu / ENTER.
Use top menu bar to navigate.
Print from *Options* header.
New Search from *Find* header.
Quit when done by using X in upper right.

Emas (EBSCO Magazine Article Summary)
Double click icon / See hourglass / Wait.
Click *Select All Databases* / ENTER
See Search Screen/ **Type** topic. (Use Boolean search
   techniques.)
Arrow down to *Limit to items with full text* (Y).
Click *F2: Search* / Wait.
Navigate the "hits" with plus key or arrow key.
Use bottom menu: *Display, Print, Escape.*

SIRS Researcher................................. ....**Double click** icon / See hourglass / Wait.
Select *Full-text articles* / ENTER.
Arrow down to *Keyword search* / ENTER.
Type your topic. (Use Boolean search techniques.) / ENTER.

From *Practical Steps to the Research Process for High School* © 1999 Libraries Unlimited. 800-237-6124.

Fig. 14-6. The Internet: Graphically Speaking

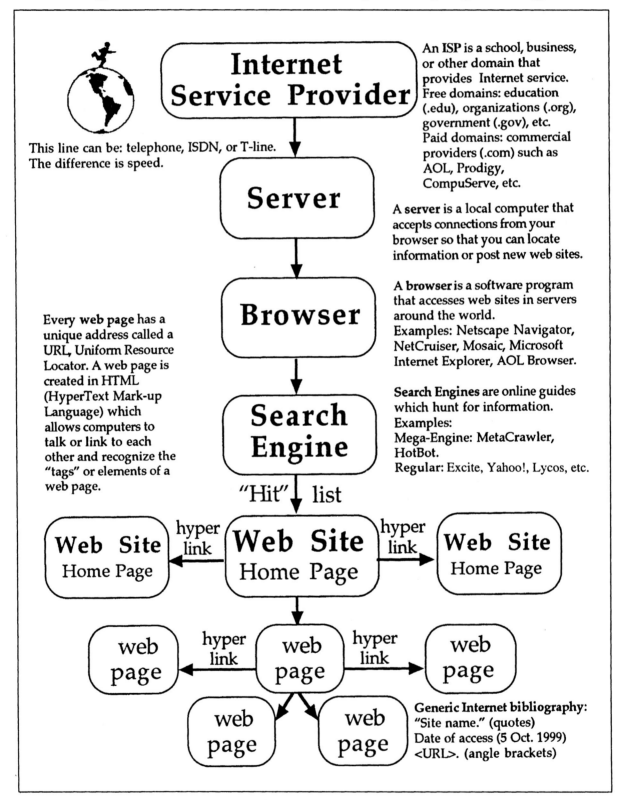

An **ISP** is a school, business, or other domain that provides Internet service. Free domains: education (.edu), organizations (.org), government (.gov), etc. Paid domains: commercial providers (.com) such as AOL, Prodigy, CompuServe, etc.

This line can be: telephone, ISDN, or T-line. The difference is speed.

A **server** is a local computer that accepts connections from your browser so that you can locate information or post new web sites.

A **browser** is a software program that accesses web sites in servers around the world. Examples: Netscape Navigator, NetCruiser, Mosaic, Microsoft Internet Explorer, AOL Browser.

Every **web page** has a unique address called a URL, Uniform Resource Locator. A web page is created in HTML (HyperText Mark-up Language) which allows computers to talk or link to each other and recognize the "tags" or elements of a web page.

Search Engines are online guides which hunt for information. Examples: Mega-Engine: MetaCrawler, HotBot. Regular: Excite, Yahoo!, Lycos, etc.

Generic Internet bibliography: "Site name." (quotes) Date of access (5 Oct. 1999) <URL>. (angle brackets)

From *Practical Steps to the Research Process for High School* © 1999 Libraries Unlimited. 800-237-6124.

The LMT's Role As Instructional Partner

The library media teacher participates in the selection, development, and promotion of excellent instructional materials. As previously discussed, the first responsibility is development of the library media center collection based on content-area, state, and district standards. Beyond the LMC, serving on site and district curriculum and instructional materials selection committees augments the LMT's ability to balance knowledge of resources against unit requirements. Such service also promotes the LMT's stature as a campus instructional mentor.

Figures 14-7 and 14-8. The Helen Keller guide sheet demonstrates that LMTs assist teachers by writing and developing instructional materials in order to adapt information literacy skills into the classroom curriculum. When a teacher comes to collaboratively plan a unit, one of the first things to be determined is the availability of information. This is why, as discussed in Chapter 4, the LMT may offer to assist the teacher in development of the unit's student topic list.

If information in certain areas is limited or unavailable, the LMT redirects or increases accessibility of information choices. To increase access, write instructional materials if necessary! The Helen Keller information gathering tool was developed for an ESL class. The teacher was ecstatic over a simple means with which his students could more understandably gather the information needed without "dumbing down" the unit requirements.

Figure 14-9. The Shakespeare Internet Bookmarks guide sheet models how LMTs enhance content-area units of study while promoting networking technologies by creating instructional materials that have an immediate and practical applicability. Using a word processing program which creates automatic "hot links" is an invaluable tool for creating student Internet worksheets. Here, the teacher of advanced placement (AP) English, whose classes were studying *Richard III*, was equally appreciative of the time invested in making available to students a highly selective group of Internet resources which exactly targeted unit information expectations. This could also be accomplished with a web site "whacking" application, the results of which could be incorporated into a specially constructed web site. Time and/or expertise likely determine which option to use.

Figure 14-10. With the CD-ROM Evaluation Form, teachers and LMTs participate in the evaluation of new instructional materials at both the site and district levels. Efficient selection of materials is extremely critical to Research Process instruction and to the budget! This form was created for a county evaluation committee primarily composed of library media teachers who wanted to provide more innovative research options not only in the library media center, but throughout their school sites and in all content areas. A simple but inclusive form was needed that would not discourage time-impacted classroom teachers from sharing their daily working knowledge of good or bad materials. Our peers are always our own best resource for new ideas and materials.

Fig. 14-7. Research Unit Adaptation for Special Students: Print Materials

Unit: Helen Keller   **Name:** _____

The purpose of this unit is to explore the resources of the library media center.

TOPIC: _____

SUBTOPICS: ◯ _____
◯ _____
◯ _____

DIRECTIONS:

1. Use the following books and resources. Record simple bibliography information.
2. Record at least 3 facts about each of the subtopics.
3. Do not repeat any information. All facts should be different.

BOOKS

Electronic card catalog:

Look up your topic in the computer. Locate a nonfiction book. Record the following:

Author: _____

Title: _____ Dewey #: _____

Record facts about your subtopics:

◯ _____
◯ _____
◯ _____

REFERENCE

Look up your topic in an encyclopedia. Record the following:

Author: _____ Article title: _____

Title: _____ Date: _____

Record facts about your subtopics:

◯ _____
◯ _____
◯ _____

From *Practical Steps to the Research Process for High School* © 1999 Libraries Unlimited. 800-237-6124.

Fig. 14-8. Research Unit Adaptation
for Special Students: Nonprint Materials

Unit: Helen Keller   **Name:** _____

CD-ROM: Record three facts about your subtopics from each of the following:

A. *World Book Multimedia Encyclopedia*

◯ _____

◯ _____

◯ _____

B. *Encarta Electronic Encyclopedia*

◯ _____

◯ _____

◯ _____

INTERNET

A. *Yahoo!* subject directory

Name of web site: _____

URL: _____

Date you found information: _____

Record three facts about your subtopics:

◯ _____

◯ _____

◯ _____

B. *Metacrawler* multi-threaded search engine:

Name of web site: _____

URL: _____

Date you found information: _____

Record three facts about your subtopics:

◯ _____

◯ _____

◯ _____

From *Practical Steps to the Research Process for High School* © 1999 Libraries Unlimited. 800-237-6124.

Fig. 14-9. Student Internet Worksheet
Adaptation for Unit Requirements

𝔖𝔥𝔞𝔨𝔢𝔰𝔭𝔢𝔞𝔯𝔢 𝔍𝔫𝔱𝔢𝔯𝔫𝔢𝔱 𝔅𝔬𝔬𝔨𝔪𝔞𝔯𝔨𝔰

1. William Shakespeare of Stratford-upon-Avon Brief History, Times and References:
   <http://www.stratford-upon-avon.co.uk/soawshst.htm>

2. The Complete Works of William Shakespeare:
   <http://www.wisdomquest.com/shakespeare.html>

3. Shakespeare's Globe: <http://www.rdg.ac.uk/AcaDepts/In/Globe/Globe.html>
   This site includes: A Virtual Tour of the Globe Theatre:
   <http://www.rdg.ac.uk/AcaDepts/In/Globe/GlobeQTVR.html>

4. The Unofficial Richard III Enthusiast's Page:
   <http://www.northcoast.com/%7Eming/richard.html>

5. Richard III "Not Guilty!" (Scroll down to trial background information.)
   <http://www.r3.or./trial/index.html>

6. Online text for Richard III:
   <http://the-tech.mit.edu/Shakespeare/History/kingrichardiii.html>

𝔗𝔢𝔞𝔠𝔥𝔢𝔯'𝔰 𝔆𝔬𝔯𝔫𝔢𝔯: Mr. Jones, English Literature, Room 100

1. *Classroom Connect*: Shakespeare lesson plan:
   <http://ctap.fcoe.k12.ca.us/ctap/shakespeare.html>

2. Shakespeare Alive! teaching materials:
   <http://www.kadets.d20.co.edu/shakespeare/shaktch.html>

3. English Literature main page:
   <http://humanitas.ucsb.edu/shuttle/english.html>

4. WWW Resources for English and American Literature:
   <http://www.indiana.edu/~libsalc/pwillett/english-www.html>

From *Practical Steps to the Research Process for High School* © 1999 Libraries Unlimited. 800-237-6124.

Fig. 14-10. CD-ROM Evaluation Form

Evaluator/Position: _____

District/School: _____

Date evaluated: _____

DISK INFORMATION

Title: _____**Copyright Date:** _____

Grade level(s): _____ **Producer:** _____

Curricular Area: ___Math ___Science ___Language Arts ___History ___Health
___PE ___ESL/SpEd ___Other (please specify): _____

Framework/Unit/Lesson Integration: _____

_____

RATING

___Highly recommended ___Recommended ___Not recommended

Check the following items, if present:

___English ___Other languages, specify:

_____

___Support materials, specify: _____

_____

___Predominance of visual images ___Predominance of text ___High interest level

___Easy to print ___Prints specific text areas ___Prints pictures ___Easy to quit

___Easy to navigate ___Quick-time movies ___Truncation ___Sound

___Bookmarks ___30-day preview ___Updates, when:_____

Contains: ___Photos, pictures ___Timelines ___Maps ___Charts

Evaluative comments:

Special features: _____

Problem areas: _____

ORDERING INFORMATION

System requirements:

Computer: _____ RAM: _____ Hard Drive: _____

Other: _____

Publisher: _____

Address: _____ Phone: _____

Catalog with competitive pricing: _____

Address: _____ Phone: _____

Price: Single user: _____ Lab pack (5): _____ Lab pack (10): _____

Site license (installed per station): ___N/A ___Yes, price: _____

Multi-user/Network (installed on server): ___N/A ___Yes, price:

From *Practical Steps to the Research Process for High School* © 1999 Libraries Unlimited. 800-237-6124.

The LMT's Role As Program Administrator

In order to teach, the LMT must have a library technician or clerk who takes over many of the daily chores of running the library media center such as: processing new materials in and old ones out, monitoring circulation, keeping inventory records, typing orders, keeping budget spreadsheets, and assisting students with nonteaching information requests. To the LMT falls the professional duty of administering one of the busiest facilities on campus by establishing policy and procedures not only for research instruction, but for budget, personnel, circulation, environment, year-end inventory, and the list goes on! How can one person wear so many hats? Dig into the technology toolbox again to build a stockpile of management helpers, freeing you to teach!

Figure 14-11. The Innovative LMC newsletter represents the advocacy role for program management. Get the word out! Here is an example of a monthly LMC newsletter that defines the mission of the library media program, outlines services and technology available for information literacy collaborative instruction, and promotes campus literacy through reading incentives. Keep the LMC an active "hub of information" through exciting and informative advertising.

Figure 14-12. This Circulation Computer direction sheet was created as a stand-up card for library science student training. The LMT can more efficiently manage personnel by creating guide sheets for using library hardware and software. Like any business manager, effective delegation of duties frees the LMT for collaborative teaching and instruction.

Figure 14-13. What better way to gain more research teaching time than to expedite processing of new materials? Training dependable students and volunteers to use guide sheets like this one called Directions: Fiction Barcodes means LMTs will no longer have to say they can't schedule teaching due to the backlog of processing.

Figure 14-14. The Sample Inventory Directions is a reminder of details forgotten from year to year. This inventory is absolutely essential to maintain an accurate electronic card catalog: the key to information access in the LMC! On-site sourcing in the Research Process is dependent on accurate search tools.

Fig. 14-11. LMC Newsletter

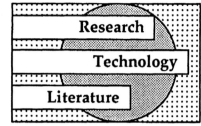

Innovative
LMC Your School
Sept. 2000

Library Media Center Mission

     We strive to be an integrated part of a school in which students, faculty, staff, parents, and community work as a team to ensure excellence in teaching and learning. The Mission of the Library Media Center Program is to ensure that all shareholders are effective users of ideas and information which is made possible by providing equal access to a variety of formats of information. To accomplish that mission, we have developed six major goals:

- Promote Information Literacy standards by providing equal opportunities for all shareholders to learn instructional strategies needed to access, evaluate, and use information.
- Promote Literacy standards by encouraging reading for both purpose and pleasure on the part of all shareholders.
- Promote Technology Proficiencies for all staff and students through the meaningful integration of technology into Standards-based units of study.
- Promote district and site educational goals through a balanced learning program that focuses on the unique academic, physical, social and emotional needs of our students.
- Incorporate community resources, including parents and local businesses, into the LMC curriculum and overall school program.
- Promote collaboration and communication among all shareholders to encourage a school climate of shared decision-making and mutual respect.

Research *instruction* ◄———

- **Sign-ups are in full swing.** Come plan collaborative research units for the upcoming semester tailored to your content area needs.

Technology *"tid-bytes"* ◄———

- **Internet access is alive and well.** Come schedule your classes for orientation and instruction. Let's plan lessons!

Literature *of the month* ◄———

- **Kick off the new year with a class orientation to this year's "Grab 'em while they're HOTs!"** Book talks now being scheduled.

INFORMATION MANAGEMENT: Access / Evaluate / Use

From *Practical Steps to the Research Process for High School* © 1999 Libraries Unlimited. 800-237-6124.

Fig. 14-12. Directions: Circulation Computer

Computerized Checkout:

1. Requires student ID.

2. Scan barcode on ID.
   (If no barcode, type in student's ID number.)

3. Check name in computer against card name.

4. Scan barcode on book.
   (Check to see if barcode is covered with tape.)

5. Hit #1 key; then hit ENTER.

6. Stamp book sticker with date stamp.
   (Add white sticker if it is missing.)

7. Desensitize book.
   (Reset Sensitize/Desensitize button if needed.)

8. Tell student to check due date.

Fines
10¢ per day—books
25¢ per day—overnight books

Book Checkout
Limit 3 books per student.
Limit 3 weeks per checkout.
Books can be renewed.

From *Practical Steps to the Research Process for High School* © 1999 Libraries Unlimited. 800-237-6124.

Fig. 14-13. Directions: Fiction Barcodes

Adult will open the circulation program, then:

1. **Press** F6.
2. **Type** barcode #34179. (This sets an easy window.)
3. **Press** F10. (This creates a new record.)
4. **Fill in** the following spaces:
    Title: not the series, but look for all real title parts.
    Author: last name, first name, and middle name or initial.
    Call number: CAPS— first three letters of author's last name.
    Pub. place: bottom of title page (first one).
    Pub. name: bottom of title page.
    Pub. date: back of title page, find *latest* date.
    Barcode #: ask adult for starting number.
    Mat. type: see "Material Types" list.
    Price: hard back is $15.00, unless stated.
        paperback is $5.00, unless stated.

PROOFREAD YOUR WORK

5. **Hit** Enter until "Subjects" box appears.
6. **Find** information with Arabic numbers on back of title page.
7. **Select** information only from the numbered items:
    Stop at apostrophe for each numbered item.
    Stop when numbers repeat or change.
8. **Type** the information for each numbered item in a different "Subjects" box.
9. **Hit** Enter for next "Subjects" box.
    Example: 1 of 1 / Enter / 2 of 2, etc.

PROOFREAD YOUR WORK

10. **Hit** Enter until screen says, "End of record."
11. **Hit** Escape / Escape.
12. **Hit** F6. Start over at number 1.

From *Practical Steps to the Research Process for High School* © 1999 Libraries Unlimited. 800-237-6124.

Fig. 14-14. Directions: Inventory (Sample)

Preinventory

1. Charge portable unit overnight.
2. Load, or check for, portable software in the computer.

I. Set up and test portable

II. Set up computer software

1. Open circulation program in computer.
2. Navigate to System Main Menu / 4 / Enter
3. Inventory software page is displayed: "Portable Circulation/Inventory."
4. Portable Communication Menu / 1 ("Transmit Data")
5. To check setup:
   A. F2 / Enter (Setup will be highlighted.)
   B. Pick up at "Configuration" box diagram.
   C. *Note:* Follow on-screen menus carefully!

III. Set up computer

1. System Main Menu / 1 / Enter (navigate)
2. Main Menu / 6 (Inventory) / Enter
3. A. Inventory Menu / 1 (Prepare for Inventory)
      Note: If screen says, "This system is not available" / Escape
      Then: 3 (cancels previous inventory data) / Enter
   B. Inventory Menu / 1 / Enter
4. Screen asks: "Limit to range?"
   If no: follow screen commands for full collection coverage.
   If yes: A. "Determine range of call numbers" (see Material Report).
            B. Select range you wish to start (6–000 recommended).
            C. Start: For example, to select 0–99:
                  Lower limit: 000.000AAA / Enter
                  Upper limit: 099.999ZZZ / Enter
            D. "Do you want to exclude any material types?" / Y / Enter
                  Note: "Y" for all materials types you're excluding.
                       "N" for the one type you want.
            E. "Inventory Menu" / Done.

IV. Set up cables

1. Computer off / portable off.
2. Female plug goes into computer port.

From *Practical Steps to the Research Process for High School* © 1999 Libraries Unlimited. 800-237-6124.

Chapter 15

Connections

"Less is more. Something as simple as the Research Process captures the complexities of educational reform."
—Deborah Stanley

Fig. 15-1. Information Literacy Standards for Student Learning

INFORMATION LITERACY

Standard 1: The student who is information literate accesses information efficiently and effectively.

Standard 2: The student who is information literate evaluates information critically and competently.

Standard 3: The student who is information literate uses information accurately and creatively.

INDEPENDENT LEARNING

Standard 4: The student who is an independent learner is information literate and pursues information related to personal interests.

Standard 5: The student who is an independent learner is information literate and appreciates literature and other creative expressions of information.

Standard 6: The student who is an independent learner is information literate and strives for excellence in information seeking and knowledge generation.

SOCIAL RESPONSIBILITY

Standard 7: The student who contributes positively to the learning community and to society is information literate and recognizes the importance of information to a democratic society.

Standard 8: The student who contributes positively to the learning community and to society is information literate and practices ethical behavior in regard to information and information technology.

Standard 9: The student who contributes positively to the learning community and to society is information literate and participates effectively in groups to pursue and generate information.

From *Practical Steps to the Research Process for High School* © 1999 Libraries Unlimited. 800-237-6124.

From *Information Power: Building Partnerships for Learning* by American Association of School Libraries and Association for Educational Communications and Technology. Copyright © 1998 American Library Association and Association for Educational Communications and Technology. Reprinted by permission of the American Library Association.

Ties to Standards, Literacy, and Information Literacy

Information Literacy

There are other teacher specialists on campus who work with the entire faculty, but the role of the library media teacher is completely unique. Like other special teachers, LMTs have their own curriculum and teaching strategies. Quite different is the importance of the collaborative process between LMTs and classroom teachers which creates a unique venue for the integration of curriculum standards, literacy, and information literacy into daily lessons using information sources, literature, and technology.

ELL/Special Modifications

Other special areas such as speech, Title I, and resource specialist/special education support regular instruction by equipping students with special strategies for mainstream learning but may not be as completely dependent on collaboration. By contrast, the information literacy curriculum of the library media program is never taught in isolation. Do not confuse the pathfinders and direction sheets that appear throughout this book with an information literacy curriculum. They are not the same! Pathfinders are merely tools to accomplish the information management strategies, the lifelong learning skills inherent in information literacy.

Content-Area Standards Related to Research

Content-Area Standard

The practical research lessons in this book have demonstrated that one of the primary roles of an effective library media teacher is to teach information literacy through collaboratively planned lessons and units based on content-area standards. This is a powerful mandate for all schools to financially support this pivotal school site instructional position. An effective library media program does nothing less than keep a school focused on standards, thereby modeling accountability strategies needed for periodic accreditation or the site review process.

Essential questions for the library media teacher to measure effective integration of curriculum standards with information literacy include the following:

- Are copies of state or district curriculum standards readily available in the library media center?

- Does the library media teacher have a good working knowledge of all standards-based units appropriate to the grade levels at the school?

- Are teacher requests for collaborative units and lessons measured against curriculum standards?

- Is the library media teacher a site and district leader in developing, promoting, and integrating curriculum standards?

- Does the LMT advocate standards-based lessons at faculty meetings, staff development presentations, and with newsletters, etc.?

- Is the purchase of LMC resources based on curriculum standards?

- Does a visually appealing library media center include displays promoting information, artifacts, and resources targeting standards-based themes and topics?

- Does the LMT/LMC sponsor promotions, events, or activities highlighting literature and technology that support standards-based themes and topics?

- Does a school site or LMC web page include a hyperlink to current district, state, and national curriculum standards?

Quintessential Literacy

Literacy

Remember the Title I reading teacher who asked, "Have all the teachers seen how this [research lesson] addresses literacy?" The Research Process embodies all aspects of literacy: reading, writing, speaking, and listening, and it easily provides opportunities for adapting each research step to accommodate high or low student literacy needs.

- **Topics** are selected or adapted based on the availability of appropriately readable information.

- **Subtopic** information must be comprehensible.

- **Sources** are matched to reading ability, language, age, and grade.

- **Reading/Thinking/Selecting** for notetaking necessitates that the student 1) has decoded (read) information, 2) has comprehended (thought about) what was read and 3) has evaluated and selected what was important to record as a note.

- **Notetaking** is the recording (writing) of information in a changed form, the criteria by which learning occurs! It is adjusted by amount and type (cards or notebook paper) to meet the needs of teacher, students, and time.

- **Sorting and Numbering** notes requires students to re-read their own material using critical thinking and evaluating strategies.

How does literacy "happen" for students in the Research Process?

Information Literacy

- **Reading:** The critical factor of information ownership occurs in the logical steps of accessing and reading information from a variety of sources, then evaluating and organizing information into notes.

- **Writing:** Notes are creatively reconstructed, through writing, into a unique paper or project.

- **Listening and Speaking:** Prewriting and composing offer opportunities for students to listen to each other speak their reports as an aid to writing. Oral reports of final products again offer speaking and listening opportunities.

Information Literacy Standards Effect Student Learning

Goals for improvement in educational achievement can be attained through collaborative efforts between the library media teacher and classroom teachers to incorporate information literacy instructional strategies in all content areas. How can this be done in a practical way? Based on the 1998 version of information literacy standards, the following list is an exercise in developing ideas to demonstrate how easy it is to adapt a wide variety of content-area lessons and activities to information literacy objectives.

Information Literacy Standards for Student Learning

From *Information Power: Building Partnerships for Learning* by American Association of School Libraries and Association for Educational Communications and Technology. Copyright © 1998 American Library Association and Association for Educational Communications and Technology. Reprinted by permission of the American Library Association.

Category I: Information Literacy

The student who is information literate:

Standard 1: Accesses information efficiently and effectively, as described by the following indicators:

1. Recognizes the need for information;
   Social science idea: Locate information for your Civil War topic which utilizes primary source information gathered from the Internet. For example, Matthew Brady photographs.

2. Recognizes that accurate and comprehensive information is the basis for intelligent decision making;
   English literature idea: Use a CD-ROM to locate information and prepare a compare/contrast discussion on the current literature topic.

3. Formulates questions based on information needs;
   Math idea: Use a word processing program to write questions for an online math chat room discussion comparing theorems.

4. Identifies a variety of potential sources of information;
   Science idea: Gather facts about diseases from three technology formats such as CD-ROM, Internet, and laser disk.

5. Develops and uses successful strategies for locating information.
   Social science idea: Use Boolean and keyword searching strategies in a favorite Internet search engine for a World War II topic.

Standard 2: Evaluates information critically and competently, as described by the following indicators:

1. Determines accuracy, relevance, and comprehensiveness;
    Business idea: Compile online Wall Street Journal *reports with those in a major newspaper to evaluate a particular corporation's track record.*

2. Distinguishes among fact, point of view, and opinion;
    English idea: Compare online sources with CD-ROM sources for reviews or criticisms of contemporary drama.

3. Identifies inaccurate and misleading information;
    Music idea: Evaluate current music web sites for facts versus opinion.

4. Selects information appropriate to the problem or question at hand.
    9th Grade CORE idea: Explore a periodical CD-ROM or the Internet for information relating to a current event.

Standard 3: Uses information accurately and creatively, as described by the following indicators:

1. Organizes information for practical application;
    Science idea: Create a chart to reflect experiment data.

2. Integrates new information into one's own knowledge;
    Business idea: Create a database of personal expenses.

3. Applies information in critical thinking and problem solving;
    Social science idea: Use CD-ROM historical information on media coverage and compare it to current journalism.

4. Produces and communicates information and ideas in appropriate formats.
    Science idea: Create a science fair project using a database and graph to plot experiment outcome data, a word processor to type the research paper, and a desktop publisher to create or include a supporting graphic image with labels.

Category II: Independent Learning

The student who is an independent learner is information literate and:

Standard 4: Pursues information related to personal interest, as described by the following indicators:

1. Seeks information related to various dimensions of personal well-being, such as career interests, community involvement, health matters, and recreational pursuits;
    Business idea: The student will use a topic-specific CD-ROM about careers to research personal career choices.

2. Designs, develops, and evaluates information products and solutions related to personal interests.

> *Specified content area: The teacher asks each student to create an electronic portfolio using HyperStudio or PowerPoint.*

Standard 5: Appreciates literature and other creative expressions of information, as described by the following indicators:

1. Is a competent and self-motivated reader;

> *English literature and special education idea: Use an electronic card catalog to search for pleasure reading selections at school or local public libraries.*

2. Derives meaning from information presented creatively in a variety of formats;

> *Art idea: The class will evaluate each others' multimedia advertisements. Required technology formats include digital cameras, laser disk or video clips, Internet downloads, and multimedia software.*

3. Develops creative products in a variety of formats.

> *Social science idea: Present a moment in history in both an oral and a written format incorporating a technology interface.*

Standard 6: Strives for excellence in information seeking and knowledge generation, as described by the following indicators:

1. Assess the quality of the process and products of personal information seeking;

> *9th Grade CORE idea: Trace your family roots through online genealogy resources.*

2. Devises strategies for revising, improving, and updating self-generated knowledge.

> *Social science idea: Work in partners or groups to create a web page on the class web site about a favorite topic in history. Update it regularly.*

Category III: Social Responsibility

The student who contributes positively to the learning community and to society is information literate and:

Standard 7: Recognizes the importance of information to a democratic society, as described by the following indicators:

1. Seeks information from diverse sources, contexts, disciplines, and cultures;

> *Social science idea: Use the Internet to conduct a comparison of human rights in countries around the world.*

2. Respects the principle of equitable access to information.

Health and special education idea: Partner with a learning or physically disabled student to do a topic search using both print and nonprint resources.

Standard 8: Practices ethical behavior in regard to information and information technology, as described by the following indicators:

1. Respects the principles of intellectual freedom;

All research classes: do not criticize topic selections of classmates.

2. Respects intellectual property rights;

All research classes: credit bibliography sources scrupulously.

3. Uses information technology responsibly.

All students sign a technology Acceptable Use Agreement in order to use school equipment to access information responsibly.

Standard 9: Participates effectively in groups to pursue and generate information, as described by the following indicators:

1. Shares knowledge and information with others;

Art idea: The student will work in a group to research and present artists from a particular style or movement using a variety of print and nonprint resources.

2. Respects others' ideas and backgrounds and acknowledges their contributions;

9th Grade CORE idea: select a partner for whom you will research and present their cultural heritage. Use a variety of print and nonprint resources.

3. Collaborates with others, both in person and through technologies, to identify information problems and to seek their solutions;

Business idea: Use an approved online chatroom to learn about current business practices and evaluate findings relative to the behavior of large corporations.

4. Collaborates with others, both in person and through technologies, to design, develop, and evaluate information products and solutions.

Computer class idea: The teacher creates two class teams who compete to learn HTML language and create the most innovative and informative web page about their high school.

Magic Bullet

The purpose of this book has been to demonstrate, in a practical way, that the Research Process embodies integrated information management to build lifelong learning skills. The Research Process truly is a magic bullet for now and the future of education. It integrates, into one neat package, almost every aspect of educational reform for which educators are and will be held accountable. It integrates both literacy and information literacy strategies and skills with content-area standards in meaningful lessons using technology proficiencies for both teachers and students. Use of process writing is an added bonus. This sounds like a huge mouthful, but in the end,

Lifelong Skills

Q: How DO you eat an elephant?
A: One bite at a time!

Bibliography

"American Psychological Association, APA PsycNET." 12 Jul. 1998
<http://www.apa.org/about/>.

Gibaldi, Joseph. *MLA Handbook for Writers of Research Papers*, fourth edition. New York: The Modern Language Association of America, 1995.

"Information Literacy Standards for Student Learning." 4 Mar. 1998
<http://www.ala.org/aasl/stndsdrft5.htm>.

"MLA Examples." 12 Feb. 1999
<http://ollie.dcccd.edu/library/Module4/M4-V/examples.htm>.

"Modern Language Association (MLA) Guide to Style." 12 Jul. 1998
<http://www.wilpaterson.edu/wpcpages/library/mla.htm>.

References

American Association of School Librarians and Association for Educational Communications and Technology for the American Library Association. *Information Power, Guidelines for School Library Media Programs.* Washington, D.C.: American Library Association, 1988.

"An Action Research Approach to Curriculum Development." 16 Dec. 1997 <http://www.shef.ac.uk/uni/academic/I-M/is/lecturer/paper2,html>.

Anderson, Mary Alice, ed. *Teaching Information Literacy Using Electronic Resources for Grades 6-12.* Worthington, OH: Linworth, 1996.

Bloom, Benjamin S., ed., et al. *Taxonomy of Educational Objectives: The Classification of Educational Goals, by a Committee and University Examiners.* New York: Longmans, Green, 1956.

California School Library Association. *From Library Skills to Information Literacy: A Handbook for the 21st Century*, 2nd edition. San Jose, CA: Hi Willow Research and Publishing, 1997.

"Computer Skills for Information Problem-Solving: Learning and Teaching Technology in Context." 19 Jun. 1998 <http://ericir.syr.edu/ithome/digests/computerskills.html>.

Eisenberg, Michael B., and Robert E. Berkowitz. "The Big Six™ & Electronic Resources: A Natural Fit." *The Book Report* Sep./Oct. 1997: 15, 22.

————. *Helping With Homework: A Parent's Guide to Information Problem-Solving.* Syracuse, NY: Eric Clearinghouse on Information & Technology, 1996.

"The Eisenberg/Berkowitz Big Six Skills© Model of Information Problem-Solving." 19 Jun. 1998 <http://ericir.syr.edu/big6/sixsteps.html>.

Farwell, Sybil. "Successful Models for Collaborative Planning." *Knowledge Quest* Jan./Feb. 1998: 24–30.

Gibaldi, Joseph. *MLA Handbook for Writers of Research Papers*, fourth edition. New York: The Modern Language Association of America, 1995.

Grover, Robert and Jacqueline McMahon Lakin, "Learning Across the Curriculum." *CSLA Journal 21/2* Vol. 21, Number 2, Spring 1998: 8–10.

"A Guide for Writing Research Papers based on Styles Recommended by The American Psychological Association." 12 Jul. 1998 <http://webster.commnet.edu/apa/apa_index.htm>.

"Harnessing the Internet: Use the *Big Six!*" 19 Jun. 1998 <http://www.clovisusd.k12.ca.us/dis...inter-snd/alta/bigsix/b6bigsix.htm>.

"Information Literacy Standards for Student Learning." 16 Dec. 1997 <http://www.ala.org/aasl/stndsdrft5.html>.

"Information Problem-Solving: The Big Six Approach to Library and Information Skills Instruction." 19 Jun. 1998 <http://www.ftn.net/~ffss/information_literacy/infops.htm>.

"Information Skills Rubric." 16 Dec. 1997 <http://www.union.k12.ia.us/ukhs/LMC/Research_Rubric.htm>.

Loertscher, David V. *Reinvent Your School's Library in the Age of Technology: A Guide for Principals and Superintendents*. San Jose, CA: Hi Willow Research and Publishing, 1997.

"Major Categories in the Taxonomy of Educational Objectives (Bloom 1956)" 19 Jun. 1998 <http://weber.u.washington.edu/~krumme/guides/bloom.html>.

Professional Growth Series. *Library Research Skills, Grades 7–12*, 2nd Edition. Worthington, OH: Linworth, 1995.

"The Role of Research in Science Teaching." 16 Dec. 1997 <http://www.nsta.org/handbook/roleres.htm>.

Shepherd, Robert D. *Writing Research Papers*. Evanston, IL: McDougal Littell, 1994.

"The Steps to the Research Cycle, Module Five." 16 Dec. 1997 <http://www.bham.webnet.edu/mod5.htm>.

Stuurmans, Harry. *Nine Steps to a Quality Research Paper*. Worthington, OH: Linworth, 1994.

Sullivan, Helen, and Linda Sernoff. *Research Reports: A Guide for Middle and High School Students*. Brookfield, CT: The Millbrook Press, 1996.

"Technology and Educational Reform." 19 Jun. 1998 <http://www.ed.gov/pubs/EdReformStudies/EdTech/>.

Index